Despair Turned into Rage
Understanding and Helping Abused, Neglected, and Abandoned Youth

Paul Lavin

Cynthia Park

Washington, DC • CWLA Press

CWLA Press is an imprint of the Child Welfare League of America. The Child Welfare League of America (CWLA), the nation's oldest and largest membership-based child welfare organization, is committed to engaging all Americans in promoting the well-being of children and protecting every child from harm.

CHILD WELFARE LEAGUE OF AMERICA, INC.
440 First Street, NW, Third Floor, Washington, DC 20001-2085
E-mail: books@cwla.org

CURRENT PRINTING (last digit)
10 9 8 7 6 5 4 3 2

Cover design by Luke Johnson

Printed in the United States of America

ISBN # 0–87868-745-9

Library of Congress Cataloging-in-Publication Data
Lavin, Paul
    Despair turned into rage :   understanding and helping abused, neglected, and abandoned youth / Paul Lavin, Cynthia Park.
        p.   cm.
    Includes bibliographical references.
    ISBN 0-87868-745-9 (alk. paper)
    1. Problem children. 2. Problem youth. 3. Depression in children--Treatment. 4. Depression in adolescence--Treatment. I. Park, Cynthia.   II. Title.
    RJ506.P63L38 1999   99-20810
    618.92'8527--dc21   CIP

Contents

Introduction

Today, more than ever, we are living in a world where youth violence is an increasingly greater problem. Those of us who work professionally or volunteer our services with troubled youth see this on a daily basis. Young people appear angrier, show greater disrespect toward authority, and display a chronic negative attitude toward those persons and institutions that try to help them. Moreover, the intensity and passion of these negative responses to life come at an earlier age. The "I don't care" proclamations of these youth, their increased use of profanity, and their manner of dress and overall deportment are often challenging and convey a clear message that they want little or nothing to do with us or what we have to offer. It is disturbing to encounter the anger in a child under 10 who appears to have no boundaries. For some youth, there seems to be no limits to their actions—up to and including homicidal and suicidal gestures.

The behavior of these blatantly recalcitrant children and adolescents can be a real turnoff to all helping persons—if we make the mistake of judging these youth only by their negative and persistent actions. The chances are that the more hardened the child, the more likely it is that he has experienced repeated abuse, neglect, or outright rejection by his own parents and/or other significant adults. The immense pain and hurt associated with these profoundly negative experiences is what we don't see. Rather, we only observe their fury and enraged demeanor, not the humiliation, degradation, and utter hopelessness paving the way toward later acting-out behavior.

Angry, enraged young people have often given up on life. They feel unloved and unwanted. Moreover, they believe that their current lives have little or no purpose and that the pursuit of future goals is useless. Why try? Why care when even those persons who have given you life value you so little?

Unfortunately, it is hate that often drives the behavioral motors of these unfortunate young people—hate of their parents for abandoning, abusing, and rejecting them; hate for their teachers, social workers, and other helping adults who "try to get into their business"; hate of themselves for being so unlovable and inadequate that even their "blood" doesn't want them; and hate of life itself, which holds so little promise. It is important to recognize, however, that this hate has a cause. It emanates from a profound loss of hope. This loss of hope, this outright despair, is the source of much of their anguish. This, in essence, is what we must help these children confront and deal with if they are to heal emotionally, behave civilly, and contribute to mainstream society.

This leads to the purpose of this book. After many years of working with foster care youth, most of whom have been abused, neglected, and abandoned, we have come to the conclusion that untreated depression is the root of much of their antisocial behavior. Our purpose, therefore, is to emphasize and focus upon the early recognition and treatment of this depression. We believe that, unless this is addressed thoroughly, the problems of these troubled youngsters are only likely to worsen and multiply.

Helping these young people to recognize and cope with their enduring sadness, however, is not an easy task. First, we live in a "quick fix" society that provides both limited time and resources for dealing with youth problems. As a result, short-term symptomatic treatments (e.g., drug therapy, incarceration, the brief therapy offered by some insurance plans, etc.) that fail to address the root causes of aberrant behavior are often advocated. Unfortunately, such approaches seldom produce those substantial changes needed for real personality growth. Therefore, the child's problems simply continue, although some of these interventions may induce more subdued behavior for a time.

Second, even those of us who work in the field can underestimate the importance of focusing on the child's depression. As indicated previously, these young people often behave in an unruly and even obnoxious fashion. It is, therefore, quite understandable that what they *do*, rather than what they *think* and *feel* becomes the focal point of our treatment. Bringing about behavioral improvement alone is often temporary and insufficient. Enduring and meaningful personality change can only occur when the child's views about self, other people, and life are altered. Learning to overcome bitterness, resentment, and helplessness is essential in finding purpose in life. We must bring about these internal changes. Such changes require dramatic shifts in thinking that come only through an intense commitment made by both the children and those who work with them. Time is crucial both to absorb and to implement lasting change. The quick fix simply doesn't work in this arena. For those of us who work directly with these youngsters, this will require an even greater degree of patience, persistence, and diligent effort. This is not an easy undertaking, given all the other demands that are placed upon our time, energies, and resources. It is, however, the only way that we can bring about the permanent fix that we seek.

Finally, the children themselves make this a difficult task. They are often markedly resistant in admitting that any form of sadness affects them. Many have built a hardened shell around themselves that protects them from facing and dealing with the pain, humiliation, and degradation stemming from their earlier years. Many young people believe that acknowledging that they are depressed would make them weak and that terrifies them. The last thing that they want to admit is vulnerability. Their attitude is a way of distancing themselves from those institutions and people who they believe could only hurt them. Why would they want to let down their defenses, when they see no advantage to doing so (and, in fact, their histories illustrate many *disadvantages*)?

Many of these children trusted adults when they were young. Unfortunately, their positive expectations often led to brutal disappointment. As a result, they develop a jaded view of the world and the people in it. Because they perceive adults as untrustworthy, they become stubborn and resistant in their interactions with them. As those who work in the field can attest, children who are offered empathy and caring seem to repeatedly bite the hand that feeds them. They can exhaust the best intentions of their caretakers. This can result in interactions that reinforce the child's perceptions of the cruelty and hostility of adults, when quite the opposite is actually the case.

With the preceding in mind, our goals for this book are as follows. First, we wanted to write a book that was drawn from our own experiences. By using actual case material and events, we hope to provide you with an in-depth understanding of how these young people think and feel and why they act as they do. As noted earlier, we particularly chose to focus upon childhood and adolescent depression, because we believe that this is responsible for much of the volatile behavior of abused, neglected, and abandoned youth. This is the key message that we hope to convey through this work.

Second, we tried to write this book so that a broad range of child care workers and lay volunteers could both understand and use it. The interviewing techniques and intervention methods that we present are relatively simple and easy to put into practice. In other words, you do not have to be a psychiatrist, psychologist, or a licensed social worker to use them. This is particularly important. Those professionals and laypersons who work with these troubled youngsters on a daily basis are most likely to have an impact on their future. Thus, for the material in this book to be of value, it must be written so that it can be of use to all of them.

Finally, we have tried to emphasize those interventions most likely to be effective in helping abused, neglected, and abandoned youth. We chose methods that are not only empirically based but practical. These are the methods that we have attempted to put into practice on a daily basis. Again, we believe that these interventions can be used by a broad range of child care workers and lay volunteers. While they require some study and training, they are not overly complex or difficult to implement.

As indicated earlier, throughout the text we have incorporated the use of actual case material to support our points and to give real life and meaning to the work that we do. Hopefully, you will find this to be of value in assisting the many troubled young people who are sorely in need of our understanding and help.

1
Sifting Through the Diagnostic Quagmire

For those of us working in foster care, our first association with a child is often through paperwork. The quality and quantity of the information we receive varies widely: Sometimes it is unobtainable, sometimes it is insufficient, and sometimes it is confusing. As we emphasized in the introduction, many case records overly focus on what the child *does* rather than the psychodynamics responsible for the behavior.

Jermaine, a 13-year-old young man, was a good example of this. Although he was small, Jermaine was extremely violent. By the time Jermaine was 11, he had been to court on numerous occasions for stealing, assault, and even for firing a loaded weapon. Fortunately, he had not killed anyone. Jermaine had become so explosive that he had been expelled from school. He had established a notorious reputation for fighting, belligerency, and "getting in your face" when he felt threatened. Jermaine's family history was littered with drug and alcohol abuse, violence, and suicide. Both of his parents had been incarcerated and Jermaine had not received adequate care for many years. Jermaine's father was currently in jail for attempted murder. His mother and her live-in boyfriend repeatedly "beat on" Jermaine whenever he behaved badly. This resulted in his being placed in the foster care system. After several unsuccessful foster family placements, Jermaine was placed in an institutional setting.

At one point, Jermaine became so uncontrollable that he was hospitalized for a brief period of time. The discharge report on Jermaine described him as being remorseless and getting pleasure out of hurting others. Moreover, the staff expected Jermaine to fail and to be incarcerated. The staff also emphasized Jermaine's violent behavior (which was understandable) and the necessity of curbing this before he actually injured himself or others.

Although the report briefly alluded to Jermaine as being sad and even hopeless, little or no mention was made of his despairing orientation about life; how he suffered from the abuse, neglect, and loss of his parents; or of his potential for engaging in suicidal behavior. No one identified his feelings and thoughts about his earlier life experiences as significant factors in his more recent behavior. These only became evident after we interviewed Jermaine. It was readily apparent that these issues were the catalyst for much of his antisocial activity.

Some of the most telling disclosures occurred when Jermaine told us that his mother and her boyfriend hurt him. Jermaine stated that he still thought about this a good deal. Jermaine claimed that he didn't understand what he could have done to deserve what they did to him. Somewhere deep in his psyche, he actually believed that he did deserve the mistreatment and that he was "personally defective." These thoughts, in turn, made him angry at himself and at his parents. He even admitted that he "went off" and became so angry in thinking about his past that he took this out on other people. In fact, Jermaine had recently assaulted a staff member who was actually trying to help him. He complained that this staff member reminded him of his mother's boyfriend and that he was "getting into my business." The cues that Jermaine used to make this assessment involved the verbal exchange with the staff member, plus such nonverbal cues as the staff member's looks, his stance, and his facial expression. Unfortunately, Jermaine was so angry and defensive, he misinterpreted this staff member's words and behavior and then overreacted.

Abused, neglected, and abandoned children consistently scan their environment for threats. It was evident that Jermaine believed that other people, particularly persons in authority, were against him. He interpreted the slightest change in a person's facial expression or body movement as a sign of hostility. Jermaine was, therefore, always hypervigilant, defensive, and ready to fight at the drop of a hat. Needless to say, we had to handle Jermaine with kid gloves.

To better understand Jermaine, we invited him to talk about his past. When we began talking about his immediate family, Jermaine started to soften—after some initial belligerency. It was evident that this subject touched him deeply. His tone of voice changed and his body became slightly less tense. Although he rarely made eye contact, we could see his eyes filling with tears. Even though his mother had neglected and abused him and he was abandoned by his father, Jermaine still loved them and wanted them as part of his life, and he was still threatened by their absence. This was particularly evident when we asked him to identify three things that he wished for the most (this technique will be described later). Jermaine's first wish was, "Me to live with my mother." His second wish was, "For my mom and dad to be together." His third wish was, "That our family would stay out of trouble." Obviously, these are not the wishes of an ordinary 13-year-old boy.

When asked to chose three people to live with him on an isolated island (this technique will be described later), Jermaine selected his mother and father and then said he had no other choices. Despite their outright abuse, neglect, and abandonment, Jermaine still wanted to be with his parents. It was evident that not being part of a caring, nurturing family still deeply troubled him. Throughout the interview, Jermaine claimed that he wanted to be at home. He worried when his mother did not contact him, and he became furious when anyone even suggested he might not be able to go back with his mother. Jermaine's longing for a stable, constant, and normal family was a consistent distraction in his life. On the one hand, he could clearly report that his parents had been abusive and neglectful and that he was angry with them. Another part of him, however, longed for the validation of the love and caring that only biological parents can provide.

Interestingly, when Jermaine was asked to spontaneously complete some partial statements with the first thought that came into his mind (this method will be discussed later), his responses, which are underlined, were as follows:

- I'm afraid <u>of big people pushing me around</u>.
- When I'm afraid <u>I get real mad and go off</u>.
- Other children <u>pick on me and pluck my nerves</u>.
- Nobody knows <u>how scared I get when they get on my nerves</u>.
- I can't understand <u>why I'm so little</u>.

Obviously, Jermaine perceived himself as vulnerable and easily preyed upon by others. His marked insecurity and fearfulness led to many of the emotional explosions that we had observed. Moreover, the loss of his family and the fact that he might never receive their love, nurture, and verification of worth had significantly impaired his self-esteem. Jermaine's negative past had left him with a forlorn sense of hopelessness about his current situation and the future. Unfortunately, despite being hospitalized and then placed in the foster care system, no one had addressed these issues with Jermaine. As a result, he was only getting worse and was always on a rampage. Jermaine was in need of psychotherapy. Unless he learned to alter his pathological views and to control his emotions more effectively, he was headed for serious trouble. In fact, as he predicted, he would probably wind up incarcerated like his parents.

Identifying the Root of the Problem

As the preceding case shows, there was a lot of useful information about Jermaine that had not been included in the discharge report from the hospital. While the report touched on Jermaine's depression and provided a diagnosis, it failed to tell us about Jermaine's perceptions of himself, his family, and his future. Once we interviewed Jermaine, we saw him in quite a different light. He was hardly the raving, maniacal sociopath that we had envisioned. Rather, Jermaine was actually a frightened, insecure little boy who had become overwhelmed by feelings of utter despair and worthlessness. Why was this information so important in understanding Jermaine? It is important precisely because it offers a cause for the behavior he displayed. Jermaine's rage was the veneer, the cover that kept the world and the people in it at bay.

It kept him isolated but, in his mind, it also offered him protection. Unfortunately, it was this veneer that most people saw and to which they responded. Unless he was able to change this (and to do so would involve dealing with the root issues troubling Jermaine), we knew that he would never get better.

Jermaine's case shows that the importance of a thorough, in-depth mental health evaluation cannot be overemphasized. This includes a detailed psychosocial history, from multiple sources if possible. An appropriate diagnosis and a detailed description of the causes of the child's acting out can be of considerable value in both understanding and helping children like Jermaine. Unfortunately, many mental health evaluations tend to confuse rather than to clarify *why* the child is enraged and behaving so poorly.

Diagnostic labels and classifications that, as noted earlier, focus on the child's aberrant behavior rather than the emotional turmoil that produces it occur with far too great a frequency. Make no mistake about it! Labels and diagnostic classifications make a difference. These often determine the modality, intensity, and duration of the interventions used to help angry and rebellious youngsters. This is a pivotal issue in the treatment of abused, neglected, and abandoned youth. If we determine that the child's problems are strictly of a behavioral nature, then we may overlook or give short shrift to examining and dealing with those emotional elements that may be actually causing and perpetuating their difficulties.

As the title of this book emphasizes, it is despair and rage of a primal nature that are the driving forces behind many children's antisocial behavior. When a person despairs, he has lost all hope. Desperate persons, according to Webster, have not only lost hope but they are "rash, reckless, frantic, extreme and often outrageous" [1949, p. 225]. Moreover, enraged individuals "experience extreme vehemence of emotion or suffering [1949, p. 698]. They are "in a fury or frenzy; rave fiercely; and also are violent, as a storm." Webster goes on to describe this violence or fury "as of a wind, sea, or fire." Such descriptions enable us to clearly envision the hopeless and tumultuous rage that ferments within the abused, neglected, and abandoned child and adolescent.

Again, it is our contention that it is this excessive emotionality and the psychodynamics causing it that must be given primary consideration if true and sustaining behavioral changes are to emerge.

What causes this rage is a loss of hope and worth—a depression that is the result of persistent abuse and neglect by significant adults in the child's life. Theories of development vary, but most respect the significance of parental relationships with children as a central factor in their ability to mature successfully. Given a diet of instability, inconsistency, lack of nurture, chaos, and emotional battering, as well as the presence of physical or sexual abuse, it is easy to imagine adverse consequences on a child. We must implement helping interventions that enable the child to become hopeful, rather than hopeless, for real personality change and better self-control to occur.

Since many child care workers have access to the youngster's mental health records, it is important that we read them with this in mind. Most of us read these records because we want to know why the child or adolescent is chronically angry and acting so poorly. Unless we have a better understanding of the diagnostic labels that are used, what they mean, and how to distinguish between them, it will be difficult to use this information effectively.

We agree that the child's behavior, because of its antisocial and disruptive nature, must be a major source of concern. This negative behavior certainly should be appropriately labeled and included as a diagnostic criterion in the child's report. It is our belief, however, that depression should be given primary or principle consideration in the child's diagnosis. It is depression that leads to the hopelessness and fury that is as violent "as wind, sea, or fire" [Webster 1949, p. 698].

Behavioral Disorders Most Frequently Attributed to Acting-Out Youth

In our experience, we have found that abused, abandoned, and neglected youth are much more frequently diagnosed with behavior-based (the focus is on how the child *acts*) rather than affect-based (the focus is on the child's *feelings*) disorders. It is quite common for the diagnoses of conduct disorder, oppositional defiant disorder, and attention-deficit/hyperactivity disorder to appear on the child's records. As we have repeatedly stressed, focusing mainly on the child's behavior is understandable, given the fact that these youngsters are defiant, frequently in conflict with authority, rude, and antisocial. It makes sense, therefore, that their behavior—rather than the psychodynamics that produced it—would be the focal point of any intervention. A simple change in behavior could lead to compliance, civility, and progress within mainstream society. Such progress would lead to positive feedback from any and all persons involved with the child. The logical progression then would be for negative behavior to decrease in the face of this increasing positive reinforcement.

Unfortunately, simply treating the behavioral symptoms of recalcitrant youth is hardly efficacious. Again, while relatively quick temporary gains might emerge, it is only by altering the child's thinking and the feelings associated with it that a sustained personality change can occur. To bring about enduring changes, therefore, depression and the dynamics from which it was spawned must be identified and altered accordingly.

The rest of this chapter will discuss conduct disorder, oppositional defiant disorder, and attention-deficit/hyperactivity disorder. You will note that each of these focuses on behavioral manifestations, rather than the cognitive and emotional factors that might have caused them.

Conduct Disorder

Conduct disorder is probably the most serious of these three disorders. If unaltered, it can lead to school suspensions or expulsion, legal problems, sexually transmitted diseases, and physical injury to self or others. Interestingly, suicidal ideation, suicidal attempts, and successfully completed suicide rates are higher than normal for youngsters diagnosed with this disorder. The diagnostic criteria for conduct disorder, taken from the *Diagnostic and Statistical Manual of Mental Disorders, Fourth Edition* (DSM-IV) are listed on the next page.

DSM-IV Diagnostic Criteria for Conduct Disorder*

- A repetitive and persistent pattern of behavior in which the basic rights of others or major age-appropriate societal norms or rules are violated, as manifested by the presence of three (or more) of the following criteria in the past 12 months, with at least one criterion present in the past 6 months.

Aggression to people and animals
- often bullies, threatens, or intimidates others
- often initiates physical fights
- has used a weapon that can cause serious physical harm to others (e.g., a bat, brick, broken bottle, knife, gun)
- has been physically cruel to people
- has been physically cruel to animals
- has stolen while confronting a victim (e.g., mugging, purse snatching, extortion, armed robbery)
- has forced someone into sexual activity

Destruction of property
- has deliberately engaged in fire setting with the intention of causing serious damage
- has deliberately destroyed others' property (other than by fire setting)

- **Deceitfulness or theft**
- has broken into someone else's house, building, or car
- often lies to obtain good or favors or to avoid obligations (i.e., "cons" others)
- has stolen items of nontrivial value without confronting a victim (e.g., shoplifting, but without breaking and entering; forgery)

---

* **Source:** *Diagnostic and Statistical Manual of Mental Disorders: Fourth Edition.* Copyright 1994 by the American Psychiatric Association. Reprinted with publisher's permission.

- **Serious violations of rules**
  - often stays out at night despite parental prohibitions, beginning before the age of 13
  - has run away from home overnight at least twice while living in parental or parental surrogate home (or once without returning for a lengthy period)
  - is often truant from school, beginning before the age of 13
- The disturbance in behavior causes clinically significant impairment in social, academic, or occupational functioning.
- If the individual is age 18 years or older, criteria are not met for antisocial personality disorder.

  Specify type based on age at onset:
  - **Childhood-onset type**: onset of at least one criterion characteristic of conduct disorder prior to age 10 years
  - **Adolescent-onset type**: absence of any criteria characteristic of conduct disorder prior to age 10 years

  Specify severity:
  - **Mild**: few if any conduct problems in excess of those required to make the diagnosis and conduct problems cause only minor harm to others
  - **Moderate**: number of conduct problems and effect on others intermediate between "mild" and "severe"
  - **Severe**: many conduct problems in excess of those required to make the diagnosis or conduct problems cause considerable harm to others

As you can see, it is no wonder that this behavior would receive such attention. It is seriously dangerous to self, others, and to society at large. But what causes a child to develop so abnormally and to become so perverted and inhuman in his or her behavior? The DSM-IV provides a clue to this in describing the predisposing factors as, "parental rejection and neglect, inconsistent child-rearing practices with harsh discipline, physical or sexual abuse, lack of supervision, early institutional living, frequent changes of caregivers .... [1994,

p. 88]. Doesn't this description fit Jermaine to a tee? Note the fact that abusive and neglectful parents set the tone for the development of a conduct disorder. Also note that, like many of the children and adolescents diagnosed with this disorder, Jermaine was suicidal. Suicide is obviously spawned by severe depression. In fact, the DSM-IV points out that conduct disorder "is symptomatic of an underlying dysfunction within the individual" [1994, p. 88]. It is our contention that it is this "underlying dysfunction" which must be addressed if personality change is to occur.

Oppositional Defiant Disorder

Oppositional defiant disorder has symptoms that are not as serious as those of conduct disorder. Nevertheless, they can cause marked problems for the child or adolescent, particularly with authority figures. The characteristics of oppositional defiant disorder are listed below.

DSM-IV Diagnostic Criteria for Oppositional Defiant Disorder*

- A pattern of negativistic, hostile, and defiant behavior lasting at least 6 months, during which four (or more) of the following are present:
  - often loses temper
  - often argues with adults
  - often actively defies or refuses to comply with adults' requests or rules
  - often deliberately annoys people
  - often blames others for his or her mistakes or misbehaviors
  - is often touchy or easily annoyed by others
  - is often angry and resentful
  - is often spiteful or vindictive

  Note: Consider a criterion met only if the behavior occurs more frequently than is typically observed in individuals of comparable age and developmental level.

---

* **Source:** *Diagnostic and Statistical Manual of Mental Disorders: Fourth Edition.* Copyright 1994 by the American Psychiatric Association. Reprinted with publisher's permission.

- The disturbance in behavior causes clinically significant impairment in social, academic, or occupational functioning.
- The behaviors do not occur exclusively during the course of a psychotic or mood disorder.
- Criteria are not met for conduct disorder, and, if the individual is age 18 years or older, criteria are not met for antisocial personality disorder.

Again, like conduct disorder, oppositional defiant disorder is described by the DSM-IV as "more prevalent in families in which child care is disrupted by a succession of different caregivers or in families in which harsh, inconsistent, or neglectful child rearing practices are common" [1994, p. 92]. Once more, this description would certainly apply to Jermaine. The DSM-IV clearly notes that family dynamics are the catalyst that can bring on this problem.

Attention-Deficit/Hyperactivity Disorder

The last behavioral disorder commonly used in the diagnosis of abused, neglected and abandoned youth is attention-deficit/hyperactivity disorder (ADHD). Youngsters diagnosed with ADHD have significant problems with impulsivity, concentration, and excessive motor activity. The failure to control these can have profoundly negative effects on the child's performance at school. The characteristics of ADHD are listed below.

DSM-IV Diagnostic Criteria for Attention-Deficit/Hyperactivity Disorder*

- Either **1** or **2**:
  1 six (or more) of the following symptoms of <u>inattention</u> have persisted for at least 6 months to a degree that is maladaptive and inconsistent with developmental level:
  Inattention
  - often fails to give close attention to details or makes careless mistakes in schoolwork, work, or other activities

---

* **Source:** *Diagnostic and Statistical Manual of Mental Disorders: Fourth Edition.* Copyright 1994 by the American Psychiatric Association. Reprinted with publisher's permission.

- often has difficulty sustaining attention in tasks or play activities
- often does not seem to listen when spoken to directly
- often does not follow through on instructions and fails to finish schoolwork, chores, or duties in the workplace (not due to oppositional behavior or failure to understand instructions)
- often has difficulty organizing tasks and activities
- often avoids, dislikes, or is reluctant to engage in tasks that require sustained mental effort (such as schoolwork or homework)
- often loses things necessary for tasks or activities (e.g., toys, school assignments, pencils, books, or tools)
- often easily distracted by extraneous stimuli
- often forgetful in daily activities

2 six (or more) of the following symptoms of <u>hyperactivity-impulsivity</u> have persisted for at least 6 months to a degree that is maladaptive and inconsistent with developmental level:

Hyperactivity
- often fidgets with hands or feet or squirms in seat
- often leaves seat in classroom or in other situations in which remaining seated is expected
- often runs about or climbs excessively in situations in which it is inappropriate (in adolescents or adults, may be limited to subjective feelings of restlessness)
- often has difficulty playing or engaging in leisure activities quietly is often "on the go" or often acts as if "driven by a motor"
- often talks excessively

Impulsivity
- often blurts out answers before questions have been completed
- often has difficulty awaiting turn
- often interrupts or intrudes on others (e.g., butts into conversations or games)

- Some hyperactive-impulsive or inattentive symptoms that caused impairment were present before age 7 years.
- Some impairment from the symptoms is present in two or more settings (e.g., at school or work and at home).
- There must be clear evidence of clinically significant impairment in social, academic, or occupational functioning.
- The symptoms do not occur exclusively during the course of a pervasive developmental disorder, schizophrenia, or other psychotic disorder and are not better accounted for by another mental disorder (e.g., mood disorder, anxiety disorder, dissociative disorder, or a personality disorder).

Again, child-rearing factors are identified as possible contributors to this disorder. The DSM-IV points out that ADHD children may have a history of child abuse and neglect, multiple foster placements, and parents diagnosed with antisocial personality disorder.

It is important to note that all three of these disorders are frequently given to abused, neglected, and abandoned children who are enraged and acting out. All three focus primarily on aberrant behavior, rather than on the emotional turmoil and the underlying psychodynamics that produce them.

Lastly, the DSM-IV clearly states that dysfunctional parents, poor and even malignant child-rearing practices, being placed in institutional settings, and frequent changes in caregivers can and do spawn marked behavioral problems. In fact, Jermaine showed many of the symptoms characteristic of all three disorders. Yet, it was Jermaine's untreated depression, not the behavior itself, that was at the root of his problems.

2
Identifying Depression and Its Conversion to Rage

It would be easy to assume that angry, defiant youth are simply choosing to be antagonistic and that they could control themselves if they really wanted to. Their rebellious attitude is, in fact, so annoying that it can arouse angry feelings within us, the very people who are motivated and trained to help them. It is not easy to overlook their repeated insults, condemnations, and the rejection of the good will that we offer to them. When they fling our best efforts back into our faces, it is only natural that we would want to retaliate in some way. Because they are so disrespectful and rude, it is difficult to believe that they are not intentionally trying "to pluck our nerves" and that severe depression is the catalyst that is responsible for their actions. This is exactly what is occurring, however. The angry, defiant attitude is only the behavioral symptom that is markedly and unmistakably imprinted upon our senses.

As has been repeatedly stated, beneath this bravado is a profound and un-remitting hopelessness that is largely responsible for the antisocial behavior of abused children. Unfortunately, many angry young people are unaware that this is the driving force behind their actions. Such unconscious awareness has vast repercussions. Persons who do not understand why they act as they do are not likely to gain control of their negative emotions and behavior. Rather, they become creatures of impulse. In the case of abused, neglected, and aban-doned foster care youth, this translates into much of the enraged, explosive types of behavior that many of us observe everyday.

The child feels; then the child reacts. There is no internal monitor or gov-ernor between emotional arousal and violent action. Thus, thinking and making choices, which are language-based processes, hardly enter into the picture. Because these processes are only marginally developed, the child can "go off" in a moment's notice. There is virtually no internal mediating force to prevent this.

For the ordinary citizen, the absence of internal control is difficult to understand. Those of us who were reared in normal, nurturing environments have acquired these controls without even recognizing that we actually learned them from the significant adults in our lives. As a result, we take their acquisition for granted. We assume that everyone ought to have learned them—and if they haven't, then it is their fault.

Getting back to depression as the root of antisocial behavior, this is not so difficult to understand if you place yourself in the child's shoes. Imagine being a child in a household where your father is either unknown, absent, or in jail. Imagine that your mother is a drug addict, an alcoholic, or a sexually promiscuous adult who sleeps with a number of male friends. Imagine being beaten, sexually or physically abused, and otherwise generally ignored and left to care for yourself during the most impressionable time of your life—the years when you need the trust, love, nurture, and verification of your parents the most. Imagine learning that your birth was simply an accident. You were conceived only out of pleasure, not because you were really wanted. In fact, the treatment that you receive confirms this every single day of your life. Then ask yourself this question: If I were this child, how would I feel?

It doesn't take a rocket scientist to answer this question. Any normal, insightful person would acknowledge that immense hurt would first emerge and that anger and eventually rage would follow. After all, when your own parents value you so little, it makes sense that marked despondency and even self-hatred would chronically trouble you. It would also follow that it is essential that the child hide the "shame" of parental disaffirmation from society at large. The end product is to try and build a strong defense that protects the child from further hurt and keeps secret the intense feelings of having been rejected because one is worthless, deficient, and somehow at fault.

For abused, abandoned, and neglected youth, becoming enraged is quite natural. It is easy for them to recognize that they have been cheated out of the fulfillment of those basic needs that are accorded to almost everyone. Despair turned into rage, as you can see, then becomes the driving force leading to repeated antisocial acts that are behavioral evidence of intense psychic trauma and pain. These acts become more habitual and pronounced with the passage of time. Eventually, they become an integral part of the child's personality makeup and occur almost automatically.

Identifying and diagnosing the depression of abused, abandoned, and neglected youth is not necessarily an easy task, because these young people are not particularly skilled at talking about or describing the emotions that are aroused within them. They have difficulty recognizing and naming feelings, particularly in recognizing and talking about sad feelings. Many of these children are able to admit that they are furious or that they have an attitude. To them, the anger and the attitude are perceived as strengths because of their intimidating qualities and the "don't tread on me" image that they convey. In light of this, it is, therefore, easier to assume that these external manifestations are simply a behavioral disorder founded on unabashed arrogance or what some people believe is "too much self-esteem." On the contrary, their behavior is actually a way of distancing themselves from the emotional pain of a traumatic childhood and an overall lack of confidence in themselves and their ability to be successful in mainstream society. But don't ever expect them to admit this!

The DSM-IV presents a number of symptoms characteristic of a depressive disorder:

- significant weight loss or gain,
- loss of interest or pleasure in almost all daily activities,
- sleeping too much or too little,
- fatigue or loss of energy,
- eating too much or too little,
- inability to think and concentrate,

- suicidal thoughts, and
- feelings of worthlessness [1994, p. 327].

It is important to note, however, that a chronically irritable mood in children and adolescents is indicative of depression as well. In fact, the DSM-IV states that depressed children and adolescents "are usually irritable and cranky as well as depressed. They have low self-esteem, poor social skills and are pessimistic" [1994, p. 347]. Moreover, the DSM-IV points out that this "irritable or cranky mood may develop rather than a sad or depressed mood" [1994, p. 321]. While the child's oppositional and antisocial actions may warrant additional diagnoses (childhood and adolescent depression may be associated with ADHD and oppositional and conduct disorders), again, it is important to note that it is depression that often is the catalyst prompting them.

Lastly, the DSM-IV points out that childhood and adolescent depression is sometimes the product of unexpressed resentment and anger. In other words, the child or adolescent tries to repress these feelings but then winds up taking them out on others who have had nothing to do with causing their problems. These angry young people are hardly able to direct their frustration to the source of their antagonism, their parents, because they may be unavailable or, more significantly, because buried deep inside is a tiny hope that they may be reunited with them. Regardless of whether the parents are available or not, these youngsters are furious with them. So everyone else around them gets dumped on.

A good example of this was a volatile 16-year-old young man named James who had been living with his relatives after his parents had abandoned him. This young man was chronically angry and even admitted that his attitude was a bad one. When we interviewed him, he acknowledged this, claiming, "I get ticked off real easy. I don't like people saying things to me. A lot of people get me mad, mad all the time." That his parents were at the source of his rage and acting out was evident as the interview progressed. He contended that his mother, who was a drug addict, "just stopped caring and left." In discussing his father, who was in jail, he contended, "I don't consider my father in my life anymore." This 16-year-old boy openly admitted that he could hardly control his anger and that he took out his frustrations on other people:

> I take a lot of things out on other people. I can't help it. I don't mean it. I try to keep my mind off the things that happened in my life. And when I try to keep it off my mind, it comes back.

As the reader can see, this young man's rage was symptomatic of the pain caused by parental rejection and abandonment. When he thought about this, it only ignited his emotional fire and he became explosive. Unfortunately, given his current state of mind, he could not control himself and was actually becoming quite dangerous.

Again, it can be too easy and simplistic to focus only on the behavioral manifestations of angry, abused, neglected, and abandoned youth without examining the psychodynamics that caused those behaviors. It is only by thoroughly investigating these dynamics that we can truly understand how depression, if untreated, leads to despair and rage. Addressing child and adolescent depression is critical in devising and formulating helping interventions that are likely to work with them. The failure to accurately diagnose and plan appropriate interventions only results in the continuation and intensification of the child's behavioral problems.

3
Getting to Know the Child

A comprehensive interview will often bring out several signs indicating that the rejections, abandonment, and abuse of parents have caused strong feelings of depression. After establishing some rapport with the child, ask why he has been placed in your facility and how he feels about this (an effective place to begin exploring the child's experience). Using such open-ended questions as, "Why have you been sent here?" enables the youngster to present his version about the reasons for the placement. Moreover, open-ended questions provide the child with the opportunity to volunteer information about his parents and other experiences associated with his abuse, neglect, and abandonment. A child who willingly gives such information is less likely to be threatened or to become defensive when more specific questions follow. Gathering information about the parents and the child's perception of them is particularly important. All abused, neglected, and abandoned youth are quite aware of the fact that it is the responsibility of their parents to care for them. They know that they ought to be reared by their "blood," not outsiders. This usually becomes painfully evident as the interview progresses.

Once the child explains why he has been placed in your facility, you can then inquire about other prior placements. The more placements, the more likely it is that little, if any, bonding has occurred. This usually results in marked mistrust and an attitude that becomes primarily directed toward people in authority. The attitude partly stems from the child's increasingly negative feelings of self-worth. Multiple placements in the child's mind means that no one is committed enough to make the effort or to take the time to rear or care about him. They also reinforce the child's perception of personal worthlessness. Obviously, the longer this has occurred, the more likely it is that hopelessness and anger will have intensified. If the child has lived with a parent(s), grandparent(s), or even a foster parent(s) for an extensive period of time, there is a better chance that some bonding has occurred. The child, therefore, is more likely to believe that someone loves or cares about him. When a youngster feels loved, there is a far greater chance that she will be less despondent and angry and more hopeful about the future. A bonding experience also enhances the development of an ability to feel empathy and concern for others, which is a basic component of socializing skills and developing into a fully functioning individual.

The preceding points become more evident when, after gathering data on the number and length of prior placements, the child is asked about his mother and father. Inquiring about where the parents reside, their current circumstances, and why the child is not living with them will usually provide much valuable information, both verbal and nonverbal. During this portion of the inquiry, it is important to observe the child's eyes, facial expression, and tone of voice. It is not unusual to see tears well up in his eyes or even for him to weep. Tears mean hurt and the pain of losing or not having parental love. The angry outbursts are a diversion. These are far more likely to be noticed. Again, the anger is superimposed on strong feelings of depression and hurt that are the root causes of the problem. This is what must be dealt with if the child is to get better.

As the interview progresses, it often becomes more noticeable that these depressed young people have such low feelings of self-worth that they do not care about themselves, their current circumstances, or their future. Their frequent "I don't care" responses when confronted with the consequences of their actions confirm this. Many of these young people truly do not care what happens to them. Why should they—when even their own "blood" has rejected them?

In fact, it is not unusual to find suicidal thoughts and attempts in their history. As the child becomes more comfortable with you, he will often talk more openly about these. One 13-year-old youngster recently told us that he was so depressed that he actually wanted to be hospitalized. He said that he could not control himself, even though he tried to do so. This young man was markedly angry and repeatedly acting out. He stated that being in foster care and away from his family only made the pain of neglect and rejection more pronounced. He admitted that he was getting worse, not better. This boy told us that he was thinking about drinking bleach to kill himself. Obviously, he was crying for help that, fortunately, we were able to provide. Other angry, volatile young people describe histories of trying to hang themselves, cutting themselves with knives or other sharp objects, overdosing on pills, or even trying to shoot themselves. These enraged young people have their whole lives in front of them. Yet, they value life so little that they are willing to end their lives long before they have even begun to live them.

Although many angry, abused, and neglected youngsters turn their rage directly against themselves making overt suicidal attempts, others engage in acts of "slow suicide." While these young people don't have a plan to directly take their lives, their impulsive pleasure seeking and "in your face" risk taking epitomizes their "I don't care" attitude about life. Drug and alcohol experimentation and abuse and sexual promiscuity are good examples. For many youngsters, such experimentation begins long before their teenage years. By the time these young people become teenagers, their experimentation has become a deeply ingrained habit that they rely on to "chill out" when adversity arises. Threatening, engaging in illegal activities, intimidation, and looking for physical confrontation are examples of such risk taking. These, too, can be a threat to life.

As noted earlier, abused, angry youngsters often try to project an image of being hard and externally tough so that they can keep the world and the people in it at bay. Inside this hardened exterior, however, their emotions are those of a vulnerable, pained child who has withdrawn and practically given up on receiving the love and nurture that all humans need to develop into civilized, caring persons. Again, the more hardened the exterior, the more likely it is that a mistrusting, despairing orientation has its foothold on the child's personality development. This, in essence, is the driving force behind his behavior.

When interviewing the child, therefore, we must ask about addictive habits, how and why they started, and why they continue to persist. Moreover, asking about the child's dress, intimidating mannerisms, and about his attitude and its purpose can be revealing. Many young people have little understanding of why they behave as they do and how their dress, mannerisms, and general overall deportment affect the views that other people have of them. Again, asking what they hope to accomplish by their actions can be quite revealing. It can provide information on how these behaviors are used as a form of protection to keep them from being overwhelmed.

Finally, toward the latter part of the interview, you should ask about the child's perception of his future. Successfully oriented people have a dream. They have goals that they want to achieve and believe they are capable of reaching them. Asking these young people what they hope to accomplish can give us a sense of whether they believe they have purpose or whether they have given up on life. A good example of the latter occurred when we interviewed a 16-year-old young man who had a chronic history of antisocial behavior. He was angry, defiant, and believed that he had no future. During the interview, he went on a verbal rampage about his parents and his hopelessness. When queried about his parents, he stated the following:

> My brother is in jail and so is my mother. My father ... I don't know where he is. If I ever see him, I'll beat him up and hurt him bad. I HATE THAT MAN!

His comments about school, his recent suspension, and his future were as follows:

> I don't care whether I got suspended. That boy was picking at me. I beat him up and he'll think before he messes with me again. I never do good in school anyway. I'm failing and

I'll always fail. I'm not all that. I DON'T CARE! GET IT! I DON'T CARE! I'm not going to be anything anyway.

While the fury of this young man was quite evident, you can easily see that he had a despairing, hopeless orientation toward life. In his mind, he has already failed and has no future. Other children report their expectation is to die through violence. There will be no future; death will come soon. Obviously, these children need considerable help. If a child has a dream and believes he has a chance of achieving it, then we have something with which to work.

Getting to know the child from his or her own point of view is essential. A good interview will enable us to begin this process. It provides useful information so that we can try to form a plan that truly addresses the child's needs. The following sample questions may be helpful in conducting the interview and gathering valuable information.

- Questions on the placement and the child's view of it:
  - Why were you referred to us?
  - What caused you to be placed at our facility?
  - Why do you think you were referred to us?
  - How do you feel about being placed here?
  - What do you think was responsible for your being placed here?
- Questions on prior placements and the child's view of them:
  - Where was your last placement? How long were you there? How did you feel about being there? What was it like? Why did you leave there? How did you feel about leaving?
  - Where were you placed before this? (same follow-up questions as above)
  - Continue the previous line of questioning to the point where the child actually resided with one or both parents or with someone who was initially responsible for his or her care.
- Questions on living with and removal from parents and family:
  - When did you last live with your parent(s)?

- How long were you with them?
- Why are you no longer living with them?
- Where are your parent(s) now?
- When was the last time you saw them?
- How do you feel about not seeing or living with them?
- What do you think about being removed from their care?
- What do you think about your mother's _____? (leaving, drug abuse, drug dealing, alcohol abuse, having her boyfriend live there, going to jail, beating you, letting her boyfriend abuse you, your mother divorcing your father, etc.)
- What do you think about your father's _____? (leaving, divorcing your mother, never marrying your mother, never being there, not knowing or ever seeing him, being in jail, not contacting you, etc.)
- Do you have brothers and sisters? How old are they? Where are they now? How do you feel about them? How do you feel about being separated from them?
- If you had three wishes, what would you wish for most of all? (This technique will be discussed later.)
- If you were on an isolated island, what three people would you choose to live with you? (This technique will be discussed later.)

- Questions about school and community:
  - What grade are you in?
  - What school do you attend?
  - How do you like school?
  - How many times have you been held back? Why?
  - How many times have you been suspended? Why? How many times have you been expelled? Why?
  - What kind of learning problems do you have?
  - What kind of behavior problems do you have? Why?
  - What are you good at in school?

- Who are your best friends? What makes them good friends to you?
- How many times have you been in trouble with the law? Why? What are your thoughts about this?
- Have you ever sold drugs? How do you feel about doing this?
- Questions about behavioral patterns and habits:
  - Do you smoke cigarettes? When did you first start? How long have you been smoking? How much do you smoke each day, each week? What are your thoughts about this habit? Why do you do it? Why don't you quit?
  - Do you smoke weed (grass, marijuana)? (same follow-up as previous question) How does this affect you?
  - Have you ever used alcohol, been drunk? (same follow-up as previous question)
  - Have you ever had sex? (same follow-up as previous question) Do you use protection? Why or why not?
  - Have you ever thought about killing yourself or ever tried it? How many times? What did you think about? How did you try it? What plan did you have or do you have now? Why do you think about killing yourself? Why did you try to kill yourself in the past? Have you ever talked to anyone about killing yourself? If not, then why? If yes, what happened after you told them?
  - Do you have any trouble sleeping? What kind of trouble? Any dreams? What happens in the dreams? What happens when you wake up? Have you ever wet the bed? Do you now? How often?
  - Do you have any eating difficulties? What kind? Why?
  - Do you have a bad temper? Why? What happens to make you "go off"?
  - I notice that you dress and act a certain way (focus on attire, pants too low, hat tipped to the side; focus on behavior and mannerisms, scowl on face, posture, movements, etc.) and that you appear angry. What do you think about my observation? When you look like this

and act this way, how do you think other people (teachers, adults, peers, community members) feel about you? How does this affect you? What do you think about this? Why?

- Have you ever had a job? When? How long? How did you do at the job? How did you like it? Why did it end?

- Questions about the future:
  - What do you think will happen if you continue to behave as you do?
  - Are there any changes that you would like to make in the future? What changes, if any?
  - If you had your life to live over, what would you do differently? Why?
  - What would you like to become in the future? Why? What do you think you need to do to achieve this? What do you think your chances are of achieving this?
  - Do you ever think you will marry? Why or why not? What kind of person would you want to marry? What qualities?
  - Do you think you will have children? How would you want your children to be treated? How would you be able to make sure that they didn't wind up in an institution like you? What plan do you have to make sure that this doesn't happen?

These are just some of the sample questions you might use to understand what is going on within the child or adolescent. Their view of current and past placements, their families, their school performance, their own behavioral patterns, and their future are critical to understanding them. As you can see, such comprehensive information can provide an in-depth insight into the feelings and thinking of enraged, abused, and neglected youth. With this kind of knowledge, you will not only understand the child, but you can then tailor interventions to address individual problems more successfully. Again, this is the only way to root out and treat the depression that is destroying the formation of a developing personality.

As we have repeatedly stated, chronic depression is a problem that plagues abused, neglected, and abandoned youth. We do not generally perceive the mood of sadness, however. Rather, we see defiance and antisocial behavior punctuated with an "I don't care" attitude. Such diagnoses as attention-deficit/hyperactivity disorder, oppositional defiant disorder, and conduct disorder are often used to describe these youth's condition. While these diagnoses are often accurate, they are not always complete.

Because diagnosis serves as the basis for formulating a treatment plan, we need techniques that clearly enable us to be as accurate as possible. We have continually stressed the importance of identifying and addressing the root causes of the child's aberrant behavior—which we believe is depression. The remaining sections of this chapter discuss three such techniques: The Three Wishes, Living Alone on a Island, and Sentence Completion.

Using the Three Wishes

The Three Wishes is a simple projective technique that we have found to be particularly effective in identifying those depressive core issues associated with the antisocial behavior of abused, neglected, and abandoned youth. It can be easily and quickly administered by social workers and other professionals, and it gives a dependable snapshot of the issues that are important to the child. In fact, we have gathered much anecdotal evidence where the child's responses to The Three Wishes clearly indicate that depression, stemming from unresolved family problems, is at the root of his or her difficulties.

We suggest the following format for administering The Three Wishes. First, ask the child whether he or she has either seen the movie or heard the story about Aladdin and the magic lamp. If the child responds in the negative, present the story. If an affirmative response is given, then say the following:

> I would like you to pretend that you are Aladdin and the genie appears to you. The genie, out of thankfulness to you for releasing him from the lamp, offers you three wishes. Keep in mind that you have only three wishes. You cannot wish for any more wishes. Again, only three wishes will be given to you. Now, think very carefully. Be serious. Remember, once you have used these up, you will never have this chance again. Think carefully. What would your first and most important wish be?

Once the child gives a first wish, encourage him or her to think carefully. Then solicit the second and third wishes. Interestingly, we have found that when we present The Three Wishes as an exercise to be taken seriously, most young people, even in their middle and late teenage years, respond accordingly. The following cases are good examples of this.

You might recall James, the volatile 16-year-old young man we referred to earlier. James admitted that he had a bad attitude. He stated that he got "ticked off" easily and that he took his anger out on other people, anger that was really directed toward his parents. You might remember that James contended, "I take a lot of things out on other people. I can't help it. I don't mean it. I try to keep my mind off the things that happened in my life. And when I try to keep it off my mind, it comes back." James' three wishes were "To have my brothers and sisters together. To have someone to take care of us, not like our mother and father. To have no problems with money and food ... we'll always be fed and have a roof over our head."

Towanda, a 13-year-old girl, had a chronic history of cursing, fighting, and oppositional behavior. She had been separated from her drug-addicted mother for five years and had been unsuccessfully placed in several foster care homes. When asked to give three wishes, Towanda's first wish was, "To go back with my mother." Her second wish was, "To see my birth father," with whom she had no contact since the age of 2. After reflecting for some time, Towanda could not even give a third wish. Finally she simply stated, "That's all."

Leroy was 10 years old when he first entered foster care. He was arrested for "busting a window." Leroy had three previous arrests and was headed toward an antisocial future. Both his mother and father were incarcerated and he was found staying in an old house. Leroy's three wishes were "To get my mom a house. To get her a big radio, some furniture, and stuff. To get me and my sister some toys."

Louis was in serious trouble with the law by age 13. He contended that he was in foster care because, "I got locked up for something I didn't do, shooting a man. I was with my friends when they did it." Louis had been arrested for selling drugs on at least three occasions and he had been charged with assault. School suspensions for fighting were also reported. According to Louis, his father was "locked up since I was five." Louis had not seen his father for years and didn't know why or where he was incarcerated. The whereabouts of Louis' mother were unknown and his sisters were in foster care as well. Louis acknowledged that he was sad, particularly about his father being in jail. His three wishes were, "To be home all the time with my family, all the time. That we live in a big house. That my father came home."

Finally, to show that even youngsters in their late teenage years can respond seriously to The Three Wishes, listen to Cory's wishes. Cory was 19 years old when The Three Wishes was administered to him. He had been in foster care for seven years. Cory had a long history of stealing, selling drugs, fighting, and being truant from school. He described both of his parents as neglecting him and his brothers and sisters. Cory's father was incarcerated and his mother's whereabouts at the time of this evaluation were unknown. Cory had two wishes. The first was, "To get my mother off the streets. She's gotten thin and stuff. She's starting to use drugs and stuff." His second wish was, "To live with my mother, father, and brothers and sisters." He didn't have a third wish. It was obvious that even at the age of 19, after many years in foster care, family issues still deeply troubled him.

While these anecdotes are only a small sample of the children who enter the foster care system, we believe that they are typical of many youngsters who have been abused, rejected, and abandoned by their parents. These young people are frequently mistrusting, defensive, hostile, and antisocial. They are often diagnosed as having a behavioral disorder. As these anecdotes show, it is unresolved emotional issues centering around their dysfunctional family life that are deeply imbedded in their minds. These young people, despite years of being separated from their parents, still feel the pain of never receiving the love, nurture, and unconditional acceptance accorded to those who are brought up in normal family environments. They instinctively know that they have been cheated out of their birthright and their anger and volatility are an out-growth of the initial despair and hopelessness that they have experienced. If we do not put this unresolved issue into the appropriate diagnostic context and deal with it, the anger of these young people eventually develops into a rage that becomes displaced onto societal institutions and its innocent citizens.

While the use of The Three Wishes is not a panacea for diagnosing all the problems of troubled youth, it can be a small but significant step in under-standing the immense sadness that is at the root of their defiance and volatil-ity. The preceding examples certainly support this hypothesis. Children who grow up in normal family environments would hardly make the selections chosen by the young people in this sample. Rather, they would wish for new toys, money, travel to special places, or even world peace. Youngsters reared in nurturing and supportive families are not preoccupied with fulfilling unmet physiological, safety, social, and emotional needs. Their psychological energy, therefore, can be directed toward the successful completion of those impor-tant developmental tasks that prepare a person to become a participant in society. Hopefully, by instituting early identification and treatment programs for foster care youth, they too can move forward, instead of being dominated by their horrendous past.

We believe that The Three Wishes is a simple but valuable technique that can be of much assistance in developing a sensitivity to hidden depression and exposing this area for appropriate treatment. It provides helping profes-sionals with four distinct advantages:

- First, it can be quickly and easily administered.
- Second, it provides specific information on those social and emotional concerns that can be blocking normal developmental growth.
- Third, it can be a valuable aid in formulating an accurate diagnosis that truly identifies the source of the child's problem.
- And fourth, it can assist us in formulating a treatment plan that ad-dresses those issues which are primarily responsible for the child's aber-rant behavior.

Using Living Alone on an Island

Another technique that we have found to be helpful in assessing who is most important in the lives of angry, abused, neglected, and abandoned youth is Living Alone on an Island. Present the following story to the children or adolescents:

> I would like you to pretend that you are living on an island in the middle of an ocean. Do you know what an island is? (If the youngster says yes, continue. If the answer is no, explain what an island is and give an example.) On this island you have everything that you could possibly want. You have all the foods that you like, including foods that will help you to always remain healthy. You'll never get sick. You have all kinds of drinks, including water. You'll never be hungry or thirsty. You have clothes, video games, TV, and every toy, game, or amusement that you could possibly desire. The weather is always good and you are safe from any possible danger. Nothing bad can ever happen to you.
>
> The only problem is that there are no people on the island. You are the only person who will ever be there. In other words, you will be absolutely alone with no one to talk to or with whom you can share your good fortune. I would like you to choose three people to live on the island with you for the rest of your life. Think carefully about this. Remember, these persons will be the only people who will ever be able to live on the island with you. No one else will ever be allowed on this island. These are the only three people you will ever see or be with. Who would you choose?

Again, with great frequency, we have found that angry, depressed youth, even adolescents in their later teenage years, choose family members, particularly those whose affections they need the most. Despite the negative impact that mothers and fathers have had on these young people, they frequently select their parents to live with them on the island for the rest of their lives. Some people, relatives particularly, may be selected because they are the only ones who have shown any kindness to the child. For example, some youngsters choose grandparents, aunts, or uncles, with whom they may have lived for a period of time, even though the children acted out and had to leave them. Even when these angry young people don't select their parents, their side comments strongly indicate that they still love and need them. They usually deny that they want to be with them or deride their parents in a contemptuous fashion, so that they don't appear vulnerable. Despite their underlying pain and resentment, however, most youngsters still choose to be with their mothers and fathers. Some sample responses of various young people who have been asked to participate in this exercise follow.

Sean, an 11-year-old boy whose mother neglected and abandoned him, chose his mother, brother, and sister to live on the island with him. Stanley, a 14-year-old boy whose mother died from a drug overdose and who was then abandoned by his father, chose his mother, his teacher, and his father. Interestingly, this young man, while angry with his parents, still selected them to be on the island. He chose a teacher, whom he described as being understanding and kind, as well. This attests to the positive impact that those outside of the family can have upon a child.

Robert, a 17-year-old antisocial young man whose parents abused drugs and were incarcerated, selected his brother, mother, and father to be on the island. He admitted to being angry with his parents because they were never married, claiming, "I think they should have been together." Another 17-year-old young man who had a similar family background made almost the same choice. He selected his mother, sister, and father to be on the island. Like Robert, his parents were never married. His father, whom he never saw, abandoned his mother during the pregnancy. Yet, he still chose his father to live on the island with him.

A 12-year-old girl, whose mother was a drug addict and who had never seen her father, chose her grandmother to be with her on the island. She contended that her grandmother was the one who took care of her in her early years. Her second choice was her sister, "'cause she's my sister, because she's the only one I ever have." Lastly, she chose her boyfriend rather than her mother, even though she claimed her mother probably loved her the most.

When it was pointed out to her that her choice of the boyfriend would mean that she would never see her mother again, she stated in an angry tone, "TOO BAD!" It was obvious that she still cared deeply for her mother but rejected her out of spite.

Lastly, another 13-year-old young man, who had been placed in numerous foster families and institutions, chose his grandmother, grandfather, and aunt to live with him. This young man was abandoned by both of his parents. Although they lived in the vicinity, they avoided contact with him and took no responsibility for his upbringing. Both of his parents were drug abusers and he was deeply resentful of them. When it was pointed out that his selection meant he would never see his parents again, his retort was, "It don't bother me!" His tone of voice and mannerisms suggested otherwise, however.

The children who did not choose their parents, when asked why they did not select them, indicated by the tone of their voice that anger and resentment were the reasons for not choosing them. It was obvious that feelings of pain and loss still plagued these youngsters, even though they were reluctant to admit this. Even young people in their later teenage years were affected. Parental abuse, neglect, and rejection were still major sore spots in their lives. Yet, despite being in foster care for several years, issues surrounding their dysfunctional families remained unresolved. They still had not come to grips with the immensely negative feelings surrounding this.

Using Sentence Completion

One other simple projective technique that can be helpful in identifying the sources of stress is Sentence Completion. While there are several commercial forms of this instrument available, you can simply present the child with made-up partial statements and ask the youngster to finish these with the first thought that enters his or her mind. This method is easy to administer and requires little effort from the child. You simply read the first part of the incomplete sentences, ask the child to finish it, and then write down the response. The sentence completion can provide a good deal of insight on what the child is thinking and feeling about family, parents, school, peers, and the future. For example, listed below are some partial incomplete sentences that might be presented:

My father _____

My mother _____

I wish _____

Life would be better if _____

My future _____

My family _____

The most important thing _____

My life _____

I feel bad _____

I get mad when _____

I get frightened when _____

Sadness _____

My brother _____

My past life _____

Love is _____

These are just a few incomplete sentences that might be presented to angry, abused, and neglected youngsters. Many others could be created and presented as well.

A good example of using the incomplete sentence and its effectiveness in gathering information occurred when we interviewed Jason, a sociopathic 15-year-old boy who had been in conflict with the law for several years. Jason told us that he had been beaten several times with an extension cord by his father and beaten up numerous times by his older brothers, one of whom was in jail. Jason had run away from home before being placed in foster care. His mother, whom he deeply loved, abandoned the family when he was 10 years old. Her whereabouts were unknown. Jason stated, "I hate my life." After his mother left, Jason tried to hang himself, but he was discovered by one of his brothers who "cut me down," but "I wish he left me alone." Listed below are some of Jason's sentence completions:

My father thinks <u>I'm crazy.</u>

My mother thinks <u>I'm stupid.</u>

My brother <u>always beats me up.</u>

I like to pretend to be <u>liked by my family.</u>

I can never <u>go home.</u>

I'd like to know <u>when I can go home.</u>

Things would be better <u>if I was home.</u>

All my life <u>I regretted being born.</u>

I often wish <u>I was dead.</u>

I am sorry <u>I never get to see my mother.</u>

I can't understand why <u>my mother and father don't love me.</u>

I feel best when <u>I'm sleeping.</u>

Too many times I <u>get into trouble.</u>

Despite his sociopathic behavior, it was evident that this young man was angry, despairing, and deeply longing for the love and nurture that his parents had never given to him. Jason had become enraged, hardened, and dangerous. Like many of the previously cited cases, however, he was really an insecure, sad little boy who had given up on life. He just didn't care anymore and he was becoming reckless. As the reader can see, his responses to these incomplete sentences confirm this. Jason was obviously in need of continuous and intense help if he were to ever get better. Again, like the preceding cases, it would be easy to overly focus on his behavior and ignore the underlying psychodynamics responsible for it.

4
Conducting the Interview

This chapter presents some examples of interviews with abused, abandoned, and neglected young people who had been placed in the foster care system. During these interviews, the counselor used many of the approaches discussed in Chapter 3. As these transcripts will show, all of these young people have several things in common. They were all engaging in antisocial, acting-out behavior, they were all hurt and angry about the way that their parents treated them, they were all despairing and were quick to lose their temper, and they were all prisoners of the past, still consumed by unresolved pain stemming from family dysfunction. You will note that at some points, the interviewer goes back over or summarizes what the child has just stated. This is done for two reasons. First, the counselor wants to make sure that she clearly understands what the child said. If there were errors in the counselor's perception, then it gives the youngster the opportunity to correct these. Second, by repeating back what the child said, the counselor hopes to show that she was listening carefully and that she takes what the child said quite seriously.

Manley

Manley was a 12-year-old boy in foster care who exhibited almost all of the characteristics of a conduct and oppositional defiant disorder. Yet, severe depression was the root of his many problems. Manley presented himself as an angry young man with an attitude. He was originally placed in the juvenile justice system because he had gotten into trouble with the law on several occasions. The interview went as follows:

Counselor (C): Manley, how long have you been here now?

Manley (M): For about a month.

C: What caused you to be referred here?

M: Me and my friend made a bomb. We was caught after my friend set it off.

C: So you and your friend made and set off a bomb. What other things did you do that caused you to get placed here?

M: I made a Molatov cocktail and it made the neighbor's grass catch on fire. I saw it on TV and I didn't know whether it would work or not.

C: So besides setting off a bomb, you burned your neighbor's grass with a Molatov cocktail. What else happened to get you here?

M: I was caught shoplifting (related how he shoplifted three times and was caught).

C: So three things occurred to get you here: setting off a bomb, starting a fire, and shoplifting. What else?

M: Nothing.

C: How about school. What happened there that might have caused you to wind up here?

M: I cut school and I got suspended (related how he was frequently truant and was suspended five times for fighting in the past year).

C: What about your parents, Manley? What happened with your mother? Why aren't you with her and your father?

M: My mother left me. I was living with my friends.

C: How come she left?

M: I have no idea. I knew she was going to leave.

C: How did you know?

M: I just knew. She was using drugs and didn't come home. I just knew.

C: What about your father?

M: He's been in jail since I was a baby.

C: Did you ever see him?

M: Yes, I saw him about 20 times—in prison.

C: How did you feel about that?

M: Upset. How would you like to see your father in prison?

Manley then described feeling sad about not having his father. He finished by saying that he loved him, "'cause he was my father. I got no other father. I can't get over that."

After asking questions about the use of drugs, alcohol, tobacco, suicidal and homicidal ideation (all answered in the negative), the counselor asked Manley if he had difficulty sleeping:

M: I have trouble sleeping.

C: How come?

M: I have bad dreams about my mom. I dreamed she didn't like me and it was my fault.

C: How do you feel about mom leaving?

M: I'm upset.

Manley went on to indicate that he was hurt and sad about mom leaving. He concluded this segment by stating, "I'm angry about her leaving me."

Manley had three wishes: "Have my family back—my mom, my dad, and my sister." When asked for a second wish, Manley said, "I don't know." After much reflection, Manley's third wish was, "To have a brother." Manley's choices of people to live on an island with him were, "Mom, dad, and my sister."

As noted earlier, Manley was angry and had been in numerous fights. When asked why he had been suspended so many times for fighting, Manley said, "Because they pick on me because I'm small. They talk about my mother, say she was a B (bitch) and a slut."

Again, the preceding interview certainly indicates that depression and feelings of abandonment and rejection form the core of Manley's problems. While Manley might be diagnosed as having a behavioral disorder, hurt feelings and rage are the driving forces behind many of his antisocial acts. This, in effect, is what must be addressed if Manley is to overcome his emotional problems and become a viable participant in mainstream society.

Samantha

Samantha is a 10-year-old girl who was referred because she had been abandoned by her mother and had been living with her uncle. The uncle's girlfriend had beaten Samantha so badly that she had to be taken to the hospital and then placed in foster care. Samantha never had contact with her father. Her mother had a history of substance abuse and according to the records, she was "hostile toward her daughter." At the time of the referral, Samantha was angry and oppositional.

Counselor (C): Samantha, tell me how come you were sent here?

Samantha (S): I don't know.

C: Where did you live before coming here?

S: With my uncle.

C: What happened while you were living there that caused you to be referred here?

S: The other girl who lived there was always telling stories, like somebody be hitting her and playing with things.

C: So there was another girl living there, and it sounds like she was telling stories about you. Where did this happen?

S: It be at my uncle's. The girl live there with me.

C: How come she was there with you at your uncle's?

S: She was my uncle's girlfriend's child. She always tell lies about me.

C: What happened when the girl told lies about you?

S: She (uncle's girlfriend) beat me. He beat me too.

C: So what happened was (counselor paraphrases and summarizes the preceding). The girlfriend and your uncle beat you, and that's why you're here?

S: That's right! He was hitting on me for no reason. He hit me hard. He always hit me up side the head with the brush!

C: Samantha, how come you weren't living with mom and dad?

S: I don't know where my mommy is. She was always doing drugs. She hit me.

C: So your mom left you. She hit you and she was doing drugs and you wound up with your uncle. What about your father?

S: I don't know who my father is.

C: How do you feel about being here?

S: I don't want to be here. I want to go home. (She then admitted that she felt like crying when we talked about home. Tears welled up in her eyes.) I want to live with my mother.

C: So even though your mother left you, you still want to live with her. What was it like living with her before you went with your uncle?

S: (Tears well up in her eyes.) She hit me in the face. Her boyfriend hit me too.

C: So mom hit you and her boyfriend hit you. Tell me about that.

S: He didn't like me. He always do things to me. He always lies and hit my mommy.

C: What kind of things did he do to you?

S: He hit me on the side of my head with his hand.

C: Did he do anything else?

S: That's all. He'd just hit me all the time and tell my mother I deserved it. He lied.

Samantha denied being homicidal or suicidal, but she did report having bad dreams: "I talk in my sleep." She then described having dreams about "people coming out of the graveyard." Samantha would wake up scared and in a cold sweat. She said that she had had these dreams for "a long time." Samantha's three wishes showed a strong need for her mother's love and nurture along with receiving the simple necessities of life:

- "To live with my mother and have her not hit on me."
- "Get me some clothes and shoes."
- "Food, good food."

The three people she chose to live on an island with were, "My mommy, my worker (social worker handling her case), and my sister." Samantha then said that her sister had been placed at another facility. She had not seen her for a long time.

Again, you can see that Samantha's family was largely responsible for her current intense anger and oppositional behavior. This child longed for fulfillment of the simplest basic human and material needs. Yet, instead of receiving this, she was abused, neglected, and finally abandoned by the most important people in her life—her mother and father. While Samantha was angry, defiant, and even antisocial, it was evident that severe trauma and depression were at the root of her many problems. Not only was she having difficulty with adults and peers, but Samantha was doing poorly in school as well. It is unlikely that Samantha would become a functional member of mainstream society unless the trend of her life was reversed.

Rhoda

Rhoda was 13 years old when she entered foster care after living with a relative for several years. Rhoda had been suspended numerous times for fighting in school, and she was defiant and uncooperative with staff.

Counselor (C): Rhoda, how long have you been here?

Rhoda (R): Four months.

C: How come you were referred here?

R: 'Cause I got suspended from school five times for fighting and my grandmother put me out. She sent me into the system.

C: How do you feel about that?

R: Mad. I don't want to be here.

C: How come you were living with your grandmother and not with your parents?

R: They split up because they was always fighting.

C: Then what happened?

R: My father took my brother and my mother took my sister and me. We went to live with my grandmother.

C: So you were living with your grandmother. You, your mother, and your sister went to live with your grandmother. How did you feel about that?

R: I didn't like it. I'm a daddy's girl. Beside, I knew my mother would run off when we went to my grandmother's house.

C: What happened?

R: She ran off. She left.

C: When was the last time you saw her?

R: 1993.

C: How do you feel about that?

R: I feel mad 'cause she never called to see us, to let us know she was all right.

C: What about your father. Why don't you see him?

R: 'Cause he works seven days a week.

C: How do you feel about not seeing your father?

R: I feel mad. He don't have enough time for me. It hurt my feelings.

Rhoda admitted that she was sad and angry about all the foster home placements that she had to endure since leaving her grandmother's house. She denied having problems sleeping and eating and she did not abuse drugs or alcohol. Rhoda was not homicidal or suicidal. She was, however, still obviously preoccupied with the breakup and loss of her family, particularly the loss of contact with her sister whom she had not seen for months. When asked to choose three people to live on an island with her, Rhoda chose her sister first, her mother second, and her father third. When asked if she would like to include more people, she went on to name all of her brothers and sisters. It was evident that her family was still important to her. Rhoda's three wishes, which further confirmed this, were, "To live back with my mother and father. To get all of us (brothers and sisters) out the system (foster care). Wish that my mother would stop using drugs."

When asked if she would like other wishes, Rhoda stated, "That's it, just three." Needless to say, like the preceding cases, Rhoda's troubles stemmed from her dysfunctional family. Despite the passage of several years, her problems were not getting better.

Robert

Robert, a 17-year-old young man, had been in the foster care system for nearly ten years. He had multiple placements in various foster and group homes, eventually running away before finally turning himself in to the police. Robert had been dealing drugs and had been shot on several occasions while engaging in drug-related activities.

Counselor (C): How did you wind up getting referred to us?

Robert (R): I turned myself back into the system and they sent me here.

C: How come you turned yourself in?

R: I had no life in the streets. If I kept doing what I was doing, I would die.

C: What were you doing?

Robert described his drug dealing, how he was shot several times, and his decision to get back into the system before it was too late.

C: What was your last placement?

R: I was at a foster home before I ran away.

C: How come you ran away?

R: The woman didn't care about us. She did it just to get paid.

C: How come you weren't living with your parents?

R: I can't go and live with my mother. She's in jail for dealing drugs.

C: What about your father?

R: I never saw him. I don't know where he is. My mother and father were never married.

C: So you did live with your mother for a time, but you've never seen your father.

R: That's right. My mother, my little sister, and me lived together.

C: Anybody else?

R: Yeah, her boyfriend was there too. We lived in his house.

C: So you, your mother, and sister all lived in your mother's boyfriend's house.

R: Yeah.

C: What did you think about that?

R: I didn't like it. I was mad. He used to kick my mother out because of her drug habit.

C: Then what happened?

R: We all left there and went to some of her girlfriends' houses, but they used drugs too.

C: So then what happened?

R: Somebody called social services and that's how we wound up in the system.

Robert denied using alcohol, but he admitted to smoking marijuana "to chill out." He reported no sleeping or eating problems. Robert was not homicidal, but did indicate he felt like killing himself—although he had no plan for doing such a thing.

Robert's three wishes were, "Me, my mother, and my little sister was closer, living together again. I was still young again as a child. I wish that I could find my father. I'd like to start my life over and I wouldn't have to go through the route that I went through."

When asked to choose three people to live on an isolated island with him, Robert chose his mother, his sister, and his father. He then added, "I want to see what my father has been through."

As the preceding clearly shows, this young man, despite never seeing his father, wanted to have a relationship with him. Even though the father had abandoned his son, it was obvious that Robert longed for his guidance and for a sense of identity that only his biological father could provide. Robert's father had played virtually no part in his life. Yet, his abandonment and continued absence still plagued him.

John

John was a 16-year-old who admitted that he had an attitude. He said that this occurred, "Because of the people I hang around with." John had no further insight into the causes of his chronic antisocial behavior. John did poorly in school and had been suspended several times for fighting. He prided himself on being hard and sported his "I don't care" attitude as though it were a badge of courage.

Counselor (C): How long have you been in the system now?

John (J): Two and a half years.

C: Where were you before you came here?

J: I was living with my aunt.

C: Why were you referred into the system?

J: I was getting into a lot of trouble. I got locked up because I had a gun in the house.

C: So you were living with your aunt before coming here. Because you were getting into trouble and had a gun, you were put into the system. Why did you have a gun?

J: I needed it for protection. Make sure nobody takes my money. You gotta watch your back from people.

C: (Recap of what John had said, focusing on how you can't trust anybody and that people are out to get you.)

J: That's right, man! You can't trust anybody.

C: What about school? How come you got suspended?

J: I cussed at the teachers ... whatever.

C: How come you didn't live with your parents?

J: I did live with my mother, but she got in trouble with drugs and got locked up. Then she had to go to be rehabbed.

C: What about your father?

J: He was locked up too. He was locked up lots of times for drugs and assault.

C: You never lived with both of your parents. How come?

J: My mother and father were never married. They never lived together.

C: So you lived with your mother. Who else was there?

J: My two brothers and my mother's boyfriend.

C: How did you feel about your mother's boyfriend living there?

J: I didn't like it.

C: How come?

J: I think my mother and father should be together.

John denied abusing drugs and alcohol but admitted to smoking some marijuana in the past. He was not homicidal but acknowledged that sometimes he didn't care whether he lived or died. He reported no sleeping or eating problems. When asked to give three wishes, however, it was evident that John was still plagued by family issues, the past, and the loss of his childhood. His wishes were, "Wish my mother never started using drugs. That my father and mother be together. All the problems I had in childhood never started."

Despite the fact that John's family problems had been horrendous, note his three choices of people to live on an isolated island with him: "My two brothers, my mother, and my father."

This case again confirms that unresolved family issues, parental neglect, and preoccupation with a lost childhood just don't go away. These issues still dominate much of John's current thinking and behavior and continue to sap the psychic and emotional energy he needs to mature and move forward. Like Robert, John had failed to overcome the legacy of adversity that his parents had heaped upon him.

Edward

Edward was a 16-year-old young man who had been in the foster care system for three years. Although Edward lived with his mother, stepfather, and three brothers for the first 13 years of his life, he left them to live with his biological father. According to Edward, he moved in with his father because his mother was so depressed that she could not cope with him and his brothers. He believed that by moving in with his biological father, he would be able to take the pressure off of her. Unfortunately, his two attempts to live with his biological father were unsuccessful. Edward then wound up living with his aunt and uncle. He eventually ran away from them, began taking drugs, and was doing poorly in school. During the course of the three years, Edward had been arrested for shoplifting and fighting. He also was hospitalized several times for attempted suicide.

Counselor (C): So Edward, how come you were sent here?

Edward (E): I ran away and was doing drugs. I was skipping school.

C: How come?

E: My aunt. She tried to take control, yells too much.

C: So you were angry with your aunt and that's what prompted you to run away. What else?

E: My uncle. He pissed me off. He never talked when I had problems and stuff. And he was my blood, she wasn't.

C: So because you were angry with your aunt and uncle, you left, used drugs, and that's what caused you to be referred here.

E: Yeah.

C: What about your parents. What happened with them?

E: I don't know where they are. I haven't talked to my mom since I was thirteen.

C: How come?

E: She was always depressed and stuff. My stepdad was never around.

C: What about your father?

E: I moved in with him and things didn't work out. That happened twice.

C: Tell me about your stepfather.

E: I didn't like him. My older brother and I weren't his real children. He treated us differently then his two kids (younger brothers from his marriage to E's mother).

C: Tell me about your use of drugs.

E: I used marijuana and cocaine after I ran away.

C: What about alcohol?

E: Yea. I started drinking a lot ... liquor and beer.

C: What about suicide? Have you ever thought about it or tried it?

E: Yeah. I was in the hospital four or five times.

C: What happened?

E: I didn't think anyone was paying attention when I was depressed and things weren't going good for me. I tried to slash my wrist.

C: How about now. Do you feel like killing yourself?

E: Not right now. I'm not depressed anymore. I try to talk about it.

C: How about sleeping and eating problems?

E: I eat all right. Sometimes I can't sleep though, or I keep waking up.

When Edward was asked to give three wishes, his selections were, "To be able to see all three of my brothers together and my mom. (long pause) To get out of the group home system. (another long pause) Be successful in my goals."

When asked to choose three people to live on an island with him, Edward's choices were, "My younger brothers, my older brother, and my girlfriend."

Interestingly, Edward's first wish was to be able to see his brothers and his mother. However, she was not selected to live on the island with him. When the counselor pointed to this inconsistency, Edward attempted to rationalize it: "I don't feel anything about her now. I have no feeling. I don't love her. She did a lot of things. She got wacky. Every little thing I did was wrong."

When the counselor again commented on the inconsistency, however, Edward said, "I'd like to see her again, see how she's doing." He then admitted that his mother's rejection hurt his feelings a lot and that he got choked up talking about this. He even contended that, following his mom's rejection, he developed an "I don't care attitude about life"

Finally, when the counselor pointed out that Edward had not chosen his father to live on the island, Edward stated, "I don't like him. He's ignorant. He abused me. He hit me. He put me down all the time." Needless to say, this case clearly points to family dysfunction as the source of this young man's depression that, in part, clearly turned into despair. Edward was angry, but he tended to internalize this rage and, as a result, had on several occasions, tried to take his own life.

Laurel

Laurel, a 15-year-old young woman who had been in the foster care system for five years, had already failed twice and was only in the seventh grade. She acknowledged that this was embarrassing. Laurel initially contended that she was placed in foster care because, "I was being bad in school. I kept getting suspended, not doing what the teacher tells me or fighting." The interview showed that her acting-out behavior, however, was only the tip of the iceberg. Family dysfunction was the cause of much negativism that was currently affecting her life.

Counselor (C): Laurel, how come you were placed in the foster care system?

Laurel (L): Like I told you when you first asked me, I was doing bad in school, fighting and stuff.

C: Where were you before you came here?

L: I was living with my cousin, her and her two kids.

C: What happened?

L: She called my social worker and told her I was doing bad in school. She lied. She said she wasn't going to call her.

C: How did you feel about that?

L: I felt bad but there was no use crying, because I wasn't going to go back anyway.

C: What do you mean you felt bad? Tell me more about that.

L: I was mad 'cause she lied to me.

C: What else?

L: I felt hurt inside, when someone doesn't want you anymore.

C: Where were you before you went to your cousin?

L: I was in a foster home with Ms. Sarah since I was ten.

C: How long were you there?

L: I don't know, almost two or three years.

C: Why did you have to leave there?

L: Because I was being bad in school.

C: How did you feel about leaving?

L: I was crying and I didn't know where else I was going. I was scared because she said I was going to get beat up anywhere else I went, and by the time I was fourteen, I'd be a junkie and a weak person.

C: It sounds like being bad in school caused a lot of problems for you. How come you were so bad in school?

L: I was being bad because I wasn't home. I was thinking about my family and stuff. I hadn't seen them in years. My cousin died and I couldn't go to the funeral. She (foster mother) wouldn't let me go. I wanted to see my family but I couldn't.

C: Who did you live with before living with Ms. Sarah?

L: I was at home living with my mother and brothers and sisters.

C: What about your father?

L: I don't know where he's at. The last time that I saw him was when I was five. He asked me what I wanted for Christmas and my birthday.

C: You haven't seen him for a long time. How do you feel about that?

L: I don't care no more. I never did. I can't remember.

C: You say you don't care about your father anymore. It sounds like he might have hurt your feelings and that you're angry with him?

L: Yeah.

C: So you do think about him. What do you think?

L: I want to see how he looks. I haven't seen him in so long. I want to see him again.

C: Why did you have to leave your mother and go into the system?

L: My mother started using drugs ever since my grandmother died. My aunt called social services.

C: How did you feel about your mother using drugs?

L: I was crying. I was walking up the stairs and I saw her doing drugs. She closed the door. I felt bad. I felt hurt inside seeing my mother do that. I went to a room with my cousins and cried.

C: What else happened with your mother? What else caused you to wind up in foster care?

L: She left us a lot. I think she'd go out and buy drugs. She got locked up and left me by myself with my brothers and sisters. I was a mother at age ten. That's when I called my aunt and social services came.

C: How did you feel about what was going on with your mother?

L: I used to say to myself if I see that stuff she be smoking, I'm going to throw it away.

Laurel denied abusing drugs or alcohol. She also denied being either suicidal or homicidal. She did, however, admit that she became depressed, claiming that this occurred when "I be thinking about the past and stuff. That's when I get migraine headaches." When asked to give three wishes, Laurel's selections were "Hope I go home for good with my family. I see my little brother and sister. (long pause) I don't know." Laurel had no third wish.

Laurel's choices of three persons to live on an island with her were "my grandmother, my uncle, and my aunt." When asked why she didn't choose her mother and father, Laurel stated, "I don't know, 'cause I don't know them." In commenting on her grandmother, uncle, and aunt, Laurel said, "I loved them so much and they loved me." Interestingly, it should be noted that Laurel's grandmother, uncle, and aunt were all deceased. Despite this, she selected them, because these were the people who showed her the most affection in her life. It was evident that she sorely missed them.

Again, we can see that Laurel is another example of acting-out behavior spawned by depression and a strong sense of loss and hopelessness. Laurel, up until her most recent placement, had been doing poorly. She had been involved in psychotherapy, however, and because of this, she started doing much better in school. Laurel's antisocial behavior clearly resulted from repression and displacing her negative emotions onto others who had nothing to do with causing her problems. She even admitted this: "I used to hold everything inside. My counselor told me to let everything out and I did and it felt better. I used to never talk to nobody."

5
Helping Interventions That Work

Before launching into a description of those helping interventions that we have found to be most successful, we would like to recap our profile of the enraged, acting-out child and adolescent who has a history of abuse, neglect, and abandonment. The purpose of this review is twofold. First, it pulls together and attempts to put into perspective much of the information that was previously presented. Second, this review provides the basis or the rationale upon which our helping interventions are founded. In other words, our helping interventions are designed to focus upon the specific problems confronting abused, neglected, and abandoned youth.

It is important to keep in mind that there is no cure for much of the cognitive, social, and emotional damage that has been inflicted upon these children in their most formative years. What we hope to accomplish is to provide them with sufficient insight and inner control so that they can effectively cope with what has happened to them. Many of these unfortunate youngsters will be haunted with unpleasant memories every day for the rest of their lives. If they are able to put these in proper perspective; overcome much of the bitterness, resentment, and humiliation associated with them; and learn to behave civilly and become citizens in mainstream society, we will have achieved our goals.

As we stated earlier, we have found that most, if not all, acting-out foster care youth began their lives as vulnerable children who were deeply scarred by the rejection, abandonment, and abuse of their parents. By neglecting and abusing their offspring, these parents inadvertently taught their children that they were of little or no value to anyone. Even basic physiological and safety needs were either ignored or inconsistently provided. How can any young person feel positively about him- or herself after being reared in such physically and emotionally impoverished conditions?

In fact, in the early and most formative years, this can only be translated into feelings of insecurity, mistrust, and a profound, unremitting sadness. Eventually this leads to a jaded view of self, the world, and the people in it. The longer that the child lives with such negativism, the more deeply ingrained it becomes. Over time, sadness becomes depression and depression deepens into despair. Unfortunately, this deterioration does not stop there. An intensifying anger begins to emerge as well. When a person, particularly a child or adolescent, comes to the conclusion that he is of no worth, he starts to hate himself and regrets the day that he was born. In fact, several of the young people whom we interviewed have actually stated this. Some youngsters turn their anger inward and attempt to kill themselves. Others rail out against adults, peers, property, and society at large. Many are both suicidal and are a danger to others. All of these youngsters, regardless of their behavioral symptoms, have one thing in common. They are despairing and enraged, believing that they have been cheated and robbed of their birthright, a nurturing and secure childhood. Who could deny that they have a point?

It is our contention that it is intense depression or despair which is the fuel that drives the engine of acting-out children and adolescents. Unless this is properly identified, acknowledged, and treated accordingly, no changes will occur. In fact, their psychic, emotional, and behavioral condition is only likely to worsen, eventually wreaking havoc on all of us.

It is also our strong belief that effective intervention requires intense, long-term treatment. The simple fact is that the children we work with have come to us after years of coping with chaos and trauma. They have only managed to survive by developing protective patterns of thinking and behaving, which they will find are unsuited to success in mainstream society. To undo or reconstruct these maladaptive habits will take significant time and energy, on the part of the child as well as the adult. In fact, even if the "fix" could happen overnight, much time would still be needed for the child to learn the new coping mechanisms and the thinking and feeling states associated with them. Without sufficient time to truly assimilate new behaviors and patterns of thinking, the old, well-learned habits will resurface and change will be impossible.

The Three Components of Successful Intervention

In light of the preceding, it is evident that consistent, caring, long-term, and high-quality intervention is necessary in helping angry, despairing youth. Obviously, assisting these unfortunate children and adolescents is going to be a trying and demanding task for those adults who are willing to face this challenge. What approaches, therefore, are most likely to be successful in reaching and changing these troubled young people?

The research clearly shows that there are three combined components needed for successful treatment [Lavin 1998, 1996; Ford 1996; Izzo & Ross 1990; Garett 1985]:

- First and foremost, forming a relationship with at least one caring adult is a necessary catalyst to personality change [Lavin 1998, 1996; Azar 1995; Shealy 1995]. It should be stressed that this relationship is the foundation upon which all growth is predicated. It can not and must not be underestimated. Without a sound, trusting relationship with at least one significant adult, progress is not likely to occur.

- Second, a change in the child's thinking about himself, other people, and life itself must occur. The child must be taught to specifically use words and language mediators to modify his unhealthy views and to control his emotions. In essence, he must learn to "talk to himself" to keep cool and to make good choices. Without such training, the child will continue to be a prisoner of unconscious, impulsive forces leading to explosive, acting-out behavior.

- Lastly, changing antisocial to prosocial behavior is essential. To become a productive citizen, the youngster must be motivated to learn those skills needed to participate effectively in mainstream society. While acting-out behavior enables a person to temporarily discharge frustration and gain attention, it hardly leads to success in the civilized world. The willingness to learn appropriate social and decision-making skills, therefore, is a necessary ingredient for effective change.

The rest of this chapter discusses the first component: forming a relationship. The other components are presented in Chapters 6 and 7.

Why Forming a Relationship Is So Difficult

First and foremost, a trusting relationship is the cornerstone upon which all successful treatment of enraged youth must begin. It is important to keep in mind that these angry youngsters generally have a hostile perception of adults. Because of the shoddy, neglectful, and abusive treatment that they have received, they do not expect adults "to look out for them." Moreover, because many of these young people have been placed in multiple foster home and group facilities, they do not expect that their relationship with adults will last. Therefore, they distance themselves and take a negative, defensive stance against adults who try to help them, even those who are obviously sincere in their effort.

In fact, a helping professional or volunteer who begins to make an impact on such a youngster might find that initially the child actually becomes more rather than less hostile. Keep in mind that this hostility is a reaction formation. When the child begins to feel a sense of closeness toward the helping person, threat or fear emerges, because the child's defensive veneer is being penetrated. In other words, the hostile exterior, which has enabled these children to distance themselves and to intimidate others, starts to crumble. This, in the child's mind, exposes old, unhealed wounds from past relationships, beginning with their parents. It makes them vulnerable. And make no mistake about it! These youngsters do not want to appear weak or vulnerable.

They will marshal all of their psychological and emotional reserves to prevent this from happening.

It is important to remember that sincere, well-meaning, warm helpers evoke conflicting feelings in mistrusting youth. These young children and adolescents really want unconditional acceptance, nurture, and support from a caring adult mentor. If they take the risk of trusting such adults, which they may have done in the past, then more hurt and disappointment might occur. In fact, they expect this to happen.

To protect themselves from experiencing further emotional pain, therefore, they take an opposite tact. They become confrontational, oppositional, and even enraged. They act like they don't care and are impervious to anything that you might say. Such recalcitrant behavior helps to replace or smother their softer feelings and prevents them from possibly getting hurt.

Unconsciously, there is another psychodynamic factor at work here. Angry, rejected youth put sincere, helping persons to the test. They try to "pluck the helper's nerves" to see if, like many other adults, the helper will chastise and abandon them. Because many adults take the child's insults and negative attitude personally, they often do become frustrated, overly confrontational, and give up. Believe it or not, this provides the youngster with some perverse consolation. It confirms, in the child's mind, that he is correct in believing that adults are against him. The child, therefore, takes this current rejection and interprets it in a way that supports his jaded view of the world and the adults in it.

The immediate benefit of such a cognitive distortion is threefold. First, it strengthens the youngster's psychological defenses, protecting him from having to face and cope with possible hurt and disappointment. Second, it makes the child appear to be invincible and in control. Third, it eliminates the necessity of dealing with a painful past history. Unfortunately, the long-term consequences of such thinking and behavior are disastrous. They prevent the child from learning from those adults who are motivated and best equipped to help him.

With the preceding in mind, therefore, it is evident that a caring, secure relationship with at least one significant adult is essential to the child's rehabilitation and growth. However, not just any adult is capable of achieving this goal. To be effective, the helper must possess certain characteristics [Lavin 1998, 1996; Shealy 1995]. These are the central ingredients upon which an effective helper-child relationship is founded. A discussion of these characteristics follows.

You must be mentally and emotionally stable.

Abused, angry youth will test your mettle. To some degree, they will take out on you what has happened to them. Insults, disrespect, a cavalier attitude and sometimes even physical aggression are not uncommon. To maintain your mental and emotional stability in the face of this adversity, you must be capable of not taking the child's negative attitude personally. In other words, you must not let the child hurt your feelings. Viewing the child's behavior as a superficial, unconscious reaction to deep emotional pain will help. Try to keep in mind that the child doesn't really mean to be antagonistic or even personally insulting. He just acts that way because he is so emotionally fragile. Remember, these children have little or no personal insight. Because they have been neglected and left to fend for themselves, they have failed to learn many of the simplest skills of ordinary living. As a result, they cannot (or can barely) control their negative emotions at this stage of their lives.

Another component of stability is the degree to which each adult working with children is aware of and has resolved emotional conflicts in his or her own personal development. Some professionals in the child care field come from abused, neglected, or abandoned homes themselves. This type of personal history can be a double-edged sword in working with these youth. Acknowledging the conflicts, challenges, and hurdles may be easier, but coping with these issues may be more complex if the adult professional's own resolution has not been successful. Each adult must be cognizant of his or her responses to youth. Helping adults must be particularly alert to areas where maintaining objectivity is especially difficult. An optimal situation would be that in which the child care professional has access to other helping professionals at times when this objectivity may be threatened. In the long term, these situations may actually assist a child in working on similar issues themselves.

There are certain statements that you might silently repeat to yourself each day to help maintain your composure. Talking to ourselves not only can help us keep "our nerves from being plucked" by the child, but also helps us to maintain the emotionally healthy outlook that is essential to achieve our goal. The following examples of some self-talk will help you to focus on the real problem and enable you to avoid taking the child's disrespect personally. An added advantage comes from using self-talk: it is easier to validate its effects and to feel confident teaching children to use the technique.

- This child's attitude is caused by abuse, rejection, and neglect. She doesn't understand this and can't help being so negative right now. If I am patient, this attitude will run its course.
- This child is testing me and trying to pluck my nerves. By being strong and enduring this test, I will actually be forging a positive relationship with this youngster.
- It's not me who abused and neglected this child. This youngster is just taking out her frustration here with me because it's a safe place to unload. She is really angry with her parents. I refuse to take this personally and let this interfere with building a solid relationship.
- It is important that I set a good example by not losing my "cool" in front of this child. By maintaining control in the face of this tirade or indifference, I am actually teaching this child that she can control herself even when she is being disrespected.
- This child hasn't got a clue as to why she is acting so foolishly. How sad it is that she has never learned the rudiments of civility.

These statements, if repeated, will help to keep our negative feelings in check and prevent us from overreacting. This is essential in maintaining our emotional stability in trying circumstances.

You must be able to accept the child as is, with no strings attached.

To be successful with abused, angry youth, you must be able to accept them unconditionally, with no strings attached. This means that regardless of the child's past behavior, current attitude, and seeming refusal to accept your good will, you must continue to show an ongoing, committed interest in helping him. To be able to keep and display a positive attitude toward the child when you are ignored or treated disdainfully is not an easy task. Such acceptance (this does not mean being a doormat for the child to wipe his feet on) is necessary, however, if we are to endure the test that we alluded to earlier. Being able to convey the notion that "I accept you no matter what" (even though we can disapprove of the child's behavior), is the foundation leading to healthy personality growth. The following self-talk statements can be helpful.

- This child has never bonded with anyone. By offering and maintaining unconditional acceptance, I am laying the foundation for developing a successful relationship with him. Without this, this youngster will never develop into a normal, civil person.

- This child is a human being who, through no fault of his own, has never been reared to be respectful and civil. He is deeply hurt and this is why he is behaving so poorly. It's his behavior, not him as a person, that's the problem.

- Children reared by parents who accept them unconditionally are provided the love, nurture, and verification that lead to normal healthy growth. This unfortunate child has received abuse, neglect, and rejection from those who were supposed to treasure him. No wonder he is so belligerent and testy. He needs unconditional acceptance now more than ever.

- I'm able to help youngsters today only because there were people in my life who accepted me when I behaved badly. When I think about it, these are the people I trusted the most and who contributed the most to my development as a person. If I am going to be of benefit to this child, I've got to give him this same acceptance, despite his attitude and belligerence.

- Being tested by this youngster means that I'm actually beginning to make an impact, even though this may not be visibly apparent. This child is actually becoming aware of the fact that my desire to help him is sincere. His attitude and negative behavior toward me is a test to see if I really mean what I say.

Besides making these statements to yourself, it would be helpful to also communicate directly to the child that despite his behavior, you genuinely care about him. It is your sincerity and genuine qualities that, if you can sustain them, will win the child over. Even when the child is behaving poorly, making comments like the following can be helpful.

- Even though you are angry with me, I still care about what happens to you. I want you to be successful.
- You have had a tough life. I understand this and want to help you to turn it around.
- I want you to do well, even though you are disrespectful to me and act like you don't care. I'm going to try to stick with you no matter what. If you walk away from my help, it will be because you are rejecting my help, not because I'm rejecting you.
- You have moved around a good deal, and as a result, it's hard to believe that anyone cares enough to stick with you. Why trust someone when this happens? I can't undo what has been done. I can only say that I do care and will do my best to help you. It's up to you whether you want to give me that chance.
- You have probably been told by other adults that they care about you, but you don't believe this anymore. You have unfortunately learned not to trust people like me. However, I do care and want to help you. Only you can decide if you want me to be of help. It's your choice, not mine.

You must be empathetic and convey this so that the child knows that you really understand.

Being empathetic means that you are able to walk in the other person's shoes. It is the capacity to feel what the other person feels and to understand his or her point of view. This skill is particularly important when working with despairing, angry youngsters.

It is helpful to ask and answer these questions, particularly when the angry youngster is displaying indifference or is on a tirade: How would I feel if I had been reared in this child's environment? How would I feel if my parents treated me the way that this child was treated?

If you are able to suspend judgment about the child's negative behavior, then it is quite easy to acknowledge that marked hurt and feelings of worthlessness would be your first reaction. This would then be followed by feelings of rage, because you had been cheated from receiving the proper care to which all children are entitled. Note that pain and hurt came first! Rage and fury follow. We are easily able to see the latter, but the former is much more difficult to identify unless we are empathetic. Empathy can only be achieved by remaining nonjudgmental and truly trying to put yourself in the child's place at this particular stage in his development.

Keep in mind that the child is just that—a child. He has neither the maturity or coping skills that you have acquired through your experience. His emotional circuits, therefore, can be easily overloaded, resulting in impulsive and even obnoxious behavior. Unlike their normal peers, abused, neglected, and abandoned youth have never really learned to acquire the emotional control and social skills that we take for granted. Again, this is important to keep in mind so that your nerves don't become easily plucked. Should this occur with too great a frequency, you will lose your capacity to empathize and any chance for a relationship will eventually be undone.

Besides being able to empathize, communicating this empathy to the child in words that he or she can understand is essential. The child needs to know that you are able to see the world from his point of view, that you can really "walk in his shoes." It is important, therefore, that you as a helper have a rich feeling vocabulary. In other words, you need to be able to identify and accurately label the various emotions that the child is experiencing and then convey these to him. Moreover, attaching these emotions to a specific event or events that triggered them is important. For example, Sam, in the course of his discussion with you, clenches his fists and begins to shout loudly while describing how his mother's boyfriend beat him and she did nothing to prevent this. Your empathetic response would be, "Sam, you're furious with your mother's boyfriend because he beat you, but you're angry with your mother as well. She didn't do anything to stop it and it's her responsibility to protect you."

You might even make another addition to the preceding, which would surely convey to the child that you really understand. The addition might be, "You know, Sam, if this happened to me, I'd be enraged too. Mothers are supposed to look out for their children." To show the child that my understanding goes even beyond this, I might also add, "You know, Sam, besides being angry, I think I'd also be deeply hurt as well. It's tough when you think that a mother prefers her boyfriend to her own son. That would really hurt my feelings."

You will note that we have not only labeled the negative emotions (e.g., rage, fury, anger), but also the specific events that spawned them (e.g., beating by boyfriend, lack of mother's intervention). Moreover, adding comments about how you would feel not only communicates a deeper understanding, but lets the child know that it is perfectly appropriate to feel this way.

Lastly, it is important to note that the helper stated that he would be "deeply hurt" as well. By saying this, we are conveying to the child that experiencing feelings of hurt makes sense, particularly in light of the fact that the mother did not care enough to protect her own child.

The helper who says that he or she would feel hurt, pain, or depression is, by adult example, telling the child that it is normal to experience these emotions. The child can then choose to acknowledge or to reject these additions to her emotional life. In this way, the child is allowed to proceed at her own pace. She can maintain control and decide how little or how much she wants to reveal. This approach makes it less likely that the youngster will feel overly threatened and defensive. Moreover, it provides the child with a safe haven to fully examine what has happened and to move forward in overcoming resentment and bitterness.

It is our experience, however, that most youngsters, once they believe that they are really understood, admit that parental abuse, neglect, and rejection are extremely painful. Acknowledging depression is a big step forward for any child and any adult trying to help them. Hence, the reader can see that empathy and the capacity to convey this to the child is critical in making progress.

You must be able to forge an alliance in which the child perceives you as working with him or her.

Angry, abused and abandoned youngsters generally perceive even well-meaning adults as the enemy. The farthest thing from their mind is forging an alliance with them. Because they have been let down numerous times by the most significant adults in their lives, they do not trust easily. Yet, having the child perceive you as someone who is both trustworthy and committed is critical. Make no mistake about it. Getting the child to accept you and to believe in your sincerity is no easy undertaking. It takes time, patience, and persistence.

When you first interview an angry, abused, and mistrusting child, you will often find that he has little insight about how his impulsive, antisocial behavior impacts on the people around them. Many young people have never thought about this and simply don't care about the effect that they have on other people. Many angry youngsters cognitively know that their behavior is either socially inappropriate or morally wrong. When asked why this is so, however, their reasoning is often shallow and quite egocentric. In other words, they will usually contend that the act is wrong because something negative might happen to them, not the other person. They hardly ever view their act as being harmful or impinging upon the rights of other people.

For example, young people will frequently contend that some act is wrong because, "I got into trouble." Note that the negative consequences following the act, which affect them personally, form the basis of their reasoning. In fact, they often cannot or do not think beyond this. If you ask them to further explain the consequences, the response is frequently, "I don't know."

In essence, these young people have hardly given much thought or been motivated to care about how their behavior affects adults and peers. They lack empathy because they, themselves, have been deprived of the love, nurture, and unconditional acceptance that enables us to become other- rather than self-centered. Forging an alliance with a trustworthy adult enables them to learn to do what is right to please others, particularly those adults who are committed to guiding them. Unless these young people learn to care about what significant others think of them, they will never be motivated to acquire those skills.

To begin the forging of an alliance, we must accept the fact that the child is egocentric, antagonistic, and mistrusting. Keep in mind that the child has not made a conscious choice to be that way. Rather, his or her personality has been formed by a combination of negative environmental experiences. In other words, these children have inadvertently been reared to be difficult. Avoid comparing them with normal peers who appear to have easily acquired the appropriate attitudes and social skills of living. To do this will only cause you to become frustrated, resentful, and judgmental. Moreover, you might then become overly critical and confrontational. This will end any chance of successfully reaching the child.

The best strategy for dealing with an egocentric, antagonistic child is to take an opposite tact. In the face of the child's attitude and recalcitrant behavior, we must emphasize patience, kindness, and understanding, as trite as those may sound. How can this be achieved? You can begin by using the skills mentioned in the discussion on empathy. You must look for ways that might enable you "to do a favor" for the child. By this, we mean going out of our way to perform some services that the child might benefit from or obtaining something the child might want but could not get without your help.

For example, one antisocial youngster with whom we worked had excellent athletic talent. Because he was so highly skilled, one of the authors offered to contact a coach at a local university to consider this boy for a college scholarship, provided that his academic performance improved. The young man listened to the offer, agreed that he would like to play college sports, and consented to the contact offer. From the tone of his voice, however, it was evident that he was skeptical that anything would come from this. After contact was made, the coach reviewed the boy's press clippings and statistics. He indicated that this young man might be capable of playing college sports if his academic performance improved. The coach even agreed to come to the school to observe and interview this young man should this occur. Moreover, the coach wrote a letter on the university's stationery indicating such. After receiving the letter, the therapist showed it to him. The boy at first appeared quite surprised, almost shocked. He then made a statement that this therapist never forgot, "You did all this for me!" This youngster could hardly believe that anyone, particularly an adult, would go out of her way for him. From this point on, an alliance was formed that led to a forward-moving relationship.

This anecdote points out that going out of your way to perform some service can have far-reaching consequences. Doing a favor for a child shows that you are willing to go beyond the limits of your job, to do the extras that require more effort and for which you get no pay. In fact, once the favor has been done it now becomes a matter of historical record, something that cannot be ignored or denied. You can then always use this as a source of leverage when the child becomes antagonistic or claims that you don't care or that you just do your job for the money.

- You can point out what you did previously. ("You're treating me rudely and acting like I don't care. Remember, two weeks ago, when I went out of my way and did _____?")
- Why you did it. ("Because I believe and have confidence in you.")
- That you really do care. ("Why would I go out of my way and do this, if I didn't care about you? There was nothing in it for me, no extra pay, only inconvenience. I did it because I care about you.")

The preceding approach is often successful because the facts speak for themselves, and because it helps the angry child to raise his level of moral reasoning in several ways. First, it teaches children that adults *can* be of benefit in helping them to improve the quality of their lives. Second, it shows that some adults will go out of their way to help and that they do sincerely care. Third, it teaches children that their behavior does have an impact on those who are trying to help them. With regard to the latter point, discussing your feelings with the child when he disrespects you clearly shows him that what he does affects others. It also teaches him about fairness and reciprocity in his relationships. This is an essential ingredient in forging an effective alliance.

Lastly, this approach works because it enables you to build a history of engaging in positive, caring acts for the child. Once trust is established, the child can actually begin to care about you—what you think, how you feel, and how you act toward him. Once an alliance is forged, the child will care whether you are disappointed in him, he will want you to be proud of what he does, and he will want to seek out your advice when adversity arises. He will think about your example and what you say before "going off," disrespecting someone in authority, or engaging in some foolish, antisocial act. You will have taught the child the beginning of empathizing with others, what it means to care about another person, and how to think in a more positive, mature fashion.

Encourage self-exploration and the acceptance of responsibility.

Once rapport is established, encourage the child to become more insightful in examining his or her feelings, thinking, and behavior. The child who is able to specifically identify his various emotions and the thoughts that these generate is more likely to be able to acquire self-control. There are numerous powerful emotions that drive the engine of the enraged child. Despair, fury, anxiety, and resentment are just a few of them. Unfortunately, most youngsters are only marginally attuned to their affective life. If they are cognizant of any of their feelings, it is usually fury, rage, and anger that they are most willing to acknowledge. Yet, it is sadness, depression, and despair that are behind the behavior that we frequently observe. Thus, helping the child to become aware of the many emotions that humans experience and how these interact with each other is the task at hand.

Because many of these children have received little cognitive stimulation, the helping adult must often begin with the basics in teaching them to understand and use feeling words appropriately. This can be accomplished by example. The helper should identify and use those words that convey the right emotion and its proper level of intensity. For instance, sad persons are "down in the dumps" and experience a genuine feeling of emptiness or loss. They are still able to perform their daily activities and relate successfully to people over the course of the day, however. Their melancholy doesn't interfere with their capacity to function. Despair, on the other hand, means that a person has lost all hope. He becomes so withdrawn or antagonistic that he is unable to successfully perform daily tasks or relate appropriately to others. Despairing people, unlike those who are sad, are continuously overwhelmed. They have lost control and don't care about their lives or what happens to them.

We might view annoyance and fury in a similar manner. A person who is annoyed is experiencing anger. The anger is not so intense, however, that he or she can't perform daily tasks and fulfill their social obligations successfully. Furious people, on the other hand, lose control. They become so enraged that they are unable to relate effectively, and they lose the capacity to be rational. Obviously, the continued, ongoing experiencing of any negative emotion can be destructive. Unfortunately, these extremes are always present with abandoned, abused and neglected youth. Thus, teaching these youngsters to identify and to control emotional extremes is critical to helping them. Teaching these children the correct vocabulary to label feelings also allows them to become more comfortable with emotions. They learn that emotions change often and that no feeling can, or should, be stamped out altogether. Emotions themselves are OK and recognizing them allows them to be dealt with appropriately.

While helping angry youth to understand that their affect is important, teaching them how their emotions are influenced by their thinking is most critical. The way that they view people, events, and life itself determines the level of emotional intensity that they experience and whether they can control their behavior. Angry, abused young people, for the most part, have never learned to put their thoughts into words. Rather, they just feel an intense emotion and then behave impulsively. There is no mediating language or governing process occurring between affect and action. This then becomes the task of the helper, to point out how specific thoughts of a negative, hopeless nature lead to despair and rage. For example, an enraged, resentful child may come to you making statements like, "I don't care. I'm not all that much anyway." A young person who repeats this over and over to herself and believes this obviously is going to experience a good deal of self-hatred. This then manifests itself through angry, arrogant, defiant, and careless behavior.

This same problem occurs with youngsters who believe that, "People don't like me. They always blame me for what happens. Other people do the same thing and they don't get into trouble." The young person who believes this will typically see hostility in others even when this does not exist. As a result, he or she will constantly be resentful and on the verge of becoming enraged over the slightest criticism or glance. Again, unless the child learns to identify counterproductive thoughts and changes these, his or her attitude will continue to cause difficulty. (More specifics on identifying and changing negative thinking will be presented latter on.)

It is important that the helper use questions that stimulate the child to think about his feelings, cognition, and behavior. For instance, asking such questions as, "How did you feel?" "What were your thoughts?" "How did you react?" achieves this goal. Moreover, questions like, "How do you think the teacher felt?" "What do you think she was thinking?" "How did she react to your behavior?" stimulate the child to examine how their actions affect other people. By answering such questions, the youngster learns to develop personal insight and how his or her behavior impacts on others. Further, skillful questioning can help the youngster to recognize the importance of taking responsibility for what happens to him or her. Ultimately, it is this attitude that is essential to achieving success.

For example, James came to us claiming that the teacher disrespected him and threw him out of class. He contended that he didn't deserve this because, "I wasn't doing nothing." James cussed out the teacher and now has been suspended "for no reason." According to him, "It's the teacher's fault."

The first step to helping James was to gather information and to try to piece together what happened. James' response to the inquiry was, "The teacher disrespected me for no reason. She threw me out of the class and I got suspended for cussing her out." The interview between the helper (H) and James (J) continued as follows:

H: So the teacher threw you out of class for no reason. What were you doing in the class?

J: Nothing. I just had my head down on the desk with my eyes closed.

H: So you had your head down on your desk with your eyes closed. Why?

J: Cause I was tired and the teacher was boring.

H: So you were feeling tired and bored. Then what happened?

J: The teacher told me to wake up and pay attention. She yelled at me.

H: So you had your head on your desk with your eyes closed while the teacher was conducting the lesson. You were tired and the material bored you. The teacher yelled at you and told you to wake up and pay attention. What did you think at that point?

J: She had no right to disrespect me. I wasn't doing nothing.

H: So you were angry at the teacher. You believed it was all right for you to be sleeping in class while she was teaching a lesson. What do you think the teacher was feeling and thinking about you?

J: She was mad. She thought I shouldn't sleep in her class. But that didn't give her the right to disrespect me in front of the class.

H: So you believe the teacher shouldn't have yelled at you. Now what do you really think about sleeping in class while the teacher is conducting a lesson?

J: I guess I shouldn't have done it even if the class is boring.

H: Good thinking. You see, you get angry because you believed that you should be able to sleep if you are tired or bored. If you think about that further, that's an insult to the teacher. It's disrespect toward her. Her job is to teach. As a student, your job is to learn. If the teacher doesn't teach and you don't learn, everybody suffers. You won't get your diploma, go to college, or get a job.

J: OK. I get it. I won't do it again.

Although it is unlikely that the child would acknowledge his or her responsibility this easily, using this line of questioning and periodically summarizing what happened can encourage him to examine himself and his behavior more objectively. It helps him to see where he is errant in his thinking and how this influences both his feelings and behaviors. Moreover, this approach makes it much more likely that the youngster will come to understand how and why he is responsible for what occurred. This acceptance of responsibility is a major step in moving forward and becoming successful.

Another example of helping the child to evaluate the influence of her thinking and behavior is illustrated with the case of Joan (J). She viewed the world as a hostile place and felt adults existed only to disappoint and deny her wants. The effect of this on her behavior is seen in the conversation below with her helper (H):

J: (in a loud voice and pacing) I never get what I want. You people always say no. What's the use of asking? If I want something I should get it.

H: (calmly) So, you feel like every adult is against you and we never let you have what you want and you are angry about that.

J: (growling) Yeah, and I really want that new outfit, but what's the use of asking when I know you'll say no.

H: Well, let's talk about that outfit and why it's important. Why don't you sit down.

J: (sits down) What's the use.

H: I think you may be doing some things that hurt your chances of getting what you want.

J: Huh?

H: Well, when you come in here and talk loud and don't stop moving, you're acting like you're angry. It makes you look like you've already been told no, and you haven't even told me what you want yet.

J: But I know you'll say no.

H: Ah, and I might not, but if you act angry and frustrated we can't talk about your request. And, you are angry when I haven't said anything yet, which makes me feel mean and less willing to listen to you.

J: So, I should come in here and beg, no way.

H: No, you could come in here, say hello, ask to talk to me for a few minutes and start by telling me about your reason for needing a new outfit.

J: Why bother, you'll just say no.

H: If we can have a discussion, you can help me understand what you want and need. You'll also get a chance to listen to me. That way the chances are better that we can work something out. If you bark and yell at me, it is true that I will be less likely to want to help you.

J: So, if I don't yell and get angry, I'll get what I want?

H: Not every time, but more often than if you start out angry.

Helping children to step outside of themselves can help them to become more aware of their impact on others. They also become more attuned to the self-fulfilling prophesy of negative expectations and negative behaviors.

Set standards or goals and expect the child to reach them.

One of the most important steps in making progress is identifying the child's strengths. These can be used to help the child to believe that he is capable—provided that he applies himself—of being successful in mainstream society. All children, even those who have grown up in the worst circumstances, have strengths upon which they can build a dream for the future. Athletic talent, artistic ability, mechanical skills, the ability to lead, theatrical talent, a pleasant smile and a friendly exterior are all strengths that can be identified and molded to achieve success.

Unfortunately, most abused, neglected, and abandoned youth hardly ever think of themselves as having any strengths. Many generally view themselves as being "not all that" and expect to fail in life. As one of our older teenage young men stated, "I want to go to college someday and be a lawyer. I'll never make it, though. I'll probably wind up dead or in jail, just like my mother and father." This young man, despite having reasonably good ability, really did believe that he would be a failure. His eyes frequently became teary when he talked about his parents, particularly his mother, who had abandoned him. Eventually, he was expelled from school, and unfortunately just as he predicted, he became a failure. Too much time had elapsed for him to believe that he was capable of becoming successful. If he had been identified and helped earlier, this might have been reversed.

What happened to this young man did not have to occur, however. Most young people like to be complimented and praised for real world accomplishments. It's simply a matter of identifying something that they could do well (this must be a true strength, something that can be proven either by a test score or some behavioral attribute that would be evident to the child once it is pointed out) and helping them to develop a short- and long-term plan that leads to a future goal. For example, if a child is artistically talented, after pointing out the evidence to support this, you could show him how this could be beneficial now and in the future. His artistic talent could be used at school for various events, projects, or contests through which he could obtain recognition. Moreover, this could eventually lead to art school admissions, becoming a commercial artist, or the pursuit of some other artistic occupation.

If a child is athletically talented, this also could reap current and future benefits. Recognition for making a team and the possibility of using this to obtain higher education could be presented. The need for improving academic performance, learning acceptable social skills, and the importance of acquiring self-control can all be tied into this as well. Again, if the child's strengths are identified and presented so that he or she clearly recognizes them, then the importance of adhering to standards of behavior (e.g., proper dress and language, etc.) and setting goals (e.g., passing all subjects with a C or better) and achieving them is more likely to make sense.

Once the child recognizes the value of his or her talent and appropriate standards and goals are determined, then you should be positive, showing confidence in the child's capacity to achieve these. Let the child know that you expect her to be successful. You expect her to make improvements, persist in the face of adversity, and to overcome obstacles. Don't settle for excuses or cop outs. State emphatically and frequently, "Your test scores and/or your past performance show that you are certainly capable of being successful. I have every confidence that you can do it, no matter what has happened. You can definitely do it if you want to!" This expression of confidence from you, the adult helper, is extremely important. Because of their horrific histories, many angry and abused youngsters tend to easily drift back into negative thinking about themselves, others, and their prospects for the future. Don't accept this! Expect the child to use his or her skills and to perform successfully. Your confidence in the child may be the needed catalyst to prevent that child from losing heart.

Be firm, be direct, and set limits. Don't be afraid to challenge and confront.

As we have said, angry, abused youngsters often display an attitude and use intimidating tactics to set themselves apart from others. Their projected arrogance, however, is simply a defensive maneuver that protects them from being overwhelmed, particularly by people in authority (who are actually a threat to them). Again, don't expect these youngsters to admit this! Their bravado is worn like a badge of courage even though it is a ruse to cover strong feelings of insecurity and mistrust. Because these young people are so thin skinned, they can "go off" at a moment's notice. In fact, their tendency to become quickly offended by so-called disrespect is unconsciously designed to instill fear into the heart of an adversary or persons in authority who can influence the course of their lives. Once more, don't expect them to understand or to admit this.

You, the helping person, have the capability to control your own potential fear. In working with angry, defiant youth, you should be able to look them in the eye. You do not have to be a 250-pound football player to do this. Rather, you need to have confidence and believe in your capacity to implement these skills. Once you have established rapport and demonstrated that you have an ongoing commitment to the child, it is unlikely that he or she will "go off" on you.

In fact, if the youngster has a history of losing his temper, then you need to discuss this with him. Point out clearly, directly, and firmly that this is something that you do not want to occur. Point out the consequences of a physical confrontation, why this would be detrimental to both of you, and why it is important that you be able to challenge and confront the child when he or she is not behaving appropriately:

> When you talk with me, I know that you are angry much of the time. You believe that many of the people in your life have treated you poorly and that even now, many adults are out to get you and make your life miserable. When you come in here with an attitude, I know that I could say things that you would find to be disrespectful. This means that you could easily "go off" on me as well. Let me make it clear that I do not want this to occur. I'm here to help you, not fight with you. In fact, fighting with you would be a stupid thing for me to do.

> Think about it. If we started fighting, you might beat me up. I'd look pretty stupid going out of here busted up. It would be embarrassing to say the least. And even if I fought with you successfully, I still might get a broken nose, a black eye, or a split lip. That would make me look stupid. Then to top it all off I'd probably lose my job, because I'm supposed to be able to control myself better than that. You see, I can't win no matter what. Moreover, you can't win either. Even if you won the fight, the chances are that you'd lose your placement here and be put in a more confined facility. You'd lose much of your freedom, possibly for a long time. That's why fighting would be a foolish choice for you.

> The other point that's bad is that we would probably never work with each other again. I want to help you (If you have done "favors" in the past, you might then cite these to prove

your point.) I think that even though you are angry, you would like this help too. After all, you have some good abilities (cite these) and you can use these to be a successful _____ (cite the dream or goals) if we work together. Think about that. Our relationship really could be of benefit to you. Why throw it away just to "go off" on me?

I need to make one last point with you. If I become a coward who is frightened because you might "go off" at any time, then I will never be able to confront you about those things that you are doing that could ruin your life. I'll have to treat you like a spoiled child rather than a mature person who is capable of understanding what I'm saying and making use of this information to improve your life. I refuse to disrespect you by treating you like a spoiled child who can't control himself. I want to tell you the truth and I want you to be strong enough to accept and handle it. Remember, I'm not your enemy. I'm an adult who wants to help you. What do you think about what I'm saying?

The question at the end of this statement provides the child with the opportunity to comment upon and to ask for more clarification on what you mean. Further discussion could then clear the air concerning differences in perception, how you can be of service to the child, and the kind of respect that you need to make the relationship work.

Most youngsters that we have encountered respond positively to the preceding approach. With the establishment of rapport, they do understand that you must set limits and that you have an obligation to challenge and confront them so that they can undo bad habits and learn to cope more effectively. This point is particularly important. Working with despairing, enraged youngsters is not a job for helping professionals and volunteers who are easily frightened and lack confidence. Not just anybody can do it. This is why it can be such a great source of pride and satisfaction.

Be nurturing and persistent in advocating for the child.

It is important to recognize that working with angry, despairing youth is like a yo-yo. There are lots of ups and downs and you will be confronted with some discouraging moments. Despairing, enraged young people often give up easily when adversity arises. Because they have a poor self-concept, they are really not confident in their capacity to be successful, particularly in accomplishing those tasks required in mainstream society. This will, therefore, require you to be persistent in two respects. You must be persistent in nurturing and supporting the child particularly in bad times, and you must be persistent in advocating for the child with teachers, principals, and other persons in authority who affect the child's life.

To persistently nurture the child means that you will have to consistently express your confidence in her capacity to be successful, even though the odds are against her. The youngster must see that you are not easily discouraged and that you believe in her. Should you lose heart, then expect that the child's failure will be imminent. Angry, despairing young people count on you more than you think. They will often look to you for inspiration when all else fails. Thus, maintaining a positive attitude yourself, even during the most difficult times, is essential to helping them through the many rough spots that are bound to arise.

Keep in mind that advocating for the child when she is doing poorly is critical. Throughout your work with these youngsters, you will find a number who do not care whether they are excluded from participation in mainstream society. These young people may fail to receive needed psychological and educational services because few people are persistent enough to make sure that they get them. Their cases can easily get caught up in the bureaucratic machinery and they can be socially promoted, suspended, or even expelled from school. Making sure that they are placed in classes and courses that are geared to their cognitive and educational capabilities is important. Without a proper education, their chances for success will be severely limited.

Make no mistake about it. Although most teachers and educators are well meaning and caring, they are overburdened and beleaguered by the system that is supposed to help them to do their jobs effectively. Just one angry, despairing child can make the teacher's job (which is already difficult), a stressful one.

Advocating for the child, therefore, is an extremely important component in helping him to overcome the many hurdles facing him. While you may annoy some adults and persons in authority with your attempt to obtain needed services, taking a stand on behalf of the youngster can make all the difference as to whether he or she succeeds or later winds up in a prison cell.

Keep one last point in mind. Because you advocate for the child, it does not mean that you approve of everything that he or she says or does. It simply means that you are trying to make sure that the child receives services and help to which he or she is entitled. When a youngster acts badly and is clearly wrong, we have an obligation to confront that child and to encourage him or her to change and to do better the next time. Once you have a solid relationship with the youngster, as pointed out previously, such confrontation is likely to bear fruit and improvement is more likely to occur.

6
Distorted Thinking

The importance of correcting the cognitive distortions of angry, despairing youth is critical if they are to overcome the past and move forward. There is considerable evidence to show that cognitive restructuring is essential to helping troubled youth [Master & Coatsworth 1998; Tate et al. 1995; Izzo & Ross 1990; Guervia & Slaby 1990; Garrett 1985]. Like forming a viable relationship, however, this is not an easy task.

One of the reasons that cognitive restructuring is so difficult is because the child is so angry and despairing to begin with that he automatically tends to interpret events in a hostile light. In other words, he tends to perceive anger and negativism in others and takes a hopeless, despairing view of life almost naturally, without any forethought or planning. His brain, in essence, is clogged with negative, excessive emotionality. The world, for him, is a fearful place and he must constantly be alert to danger. Getting the child to examine his thoughts and to try to "unclog" his brain is the difficult task at hand.

A second reason why this undertaking is problematic is because the child's views are partially true. They have some validity. It is important, therefore, to acknowledge this. Such recognition makes it less likely that you will be confronted with resistance when you present new ideas. If the child perceives you as being understanding, he or she is more likely to be open to what you have to say. Your demonstrated empathy helps to unclog or diffuse automatic excessive emotionality and defensiveness. The absence of this interfering "gunk" then enables the child to process the new, beneficial information needed for gaining self-control and making better choices.

There are a number of cognitive distortions that particularly apply to angry, despairing children. As noted earlier, their thoughts usually generate feelings of resentment, rage, despair, and hopelessness. The thoughts that produce excessive negative emotionality are what we call *violpathic ideations* [Lavin 1998, 1996]. Violpathic ideations are pathological thoughts that lead to resentment, rage, and potential violent behavior. They tend to be somewhat general and global in nature, which encourages the child to perceive all experiences as "black or white," without shades of grey or exceptions. Obviously, these must be changed if the child is to make progress. Violpathic ideations, because they are so counterproductive, must be replaced by what we call *sociorespective ideations*, which are thoughts that are reality based, sensible, somewhat specific, and generally positive in their orientation. These are more likely to enable the child to gain and maintain self-control, to relate appropriately to others, to examine situations and to achieve respect. The following is a discussion of the most common violpathic ideations (VP) that we have encountered and the sociorespective ideations (SR) that we have used to challenge them.

VP1.   Parents, teachers, and social workers have messed me up. They didn't look out for me. They are responsible for my problems.

SR1.   You're angry because you believe that your parents, teachers, and social workers didn't help you when you needed it. Now you have major problems in your life. What you are saying has some truth to it. Some adults did not look out for you in your early years. This is partly responsible for your problems. However, there is nothing that you can do about their past failures. You must now choose to be consumed by hurt, hatred, and resentment—or you must try to move forward. If you stay angry and bitter, nothing will get better. If you make the effort, you can overcome your problems and you have a chance of being successful.

VP2.   Adults can't be trusted. They always let you down. It's better to keep your guard up so that you can keep from getting hurt.

SR2. You mistrust adults because in the past they were not there when you needed them. It's understandable that you do not trust them now. However, because you have had bad experiences with *some* adults, it doesn't mean that *all* adults can't be trusted. In fact, there are adults who could care about you if you gave them a chance. If you don't trust some older people, you can only learn from your friends or by experience. This could cause you to make mistakes that could be avoided. Many adults have acquired wisdom from life's experiences and want to share this with young people. If you are willing to trust them, they can help you to make good decisions because they have already faced and coped with many problems. This could help you to avoid making bad choices that could jeopardize your future.

VP3. School and work are boring. If something doesn't interest me, I shouldn't have to do it.

SR3. You resent having to work at things that don't interest you. You believe that you shouldn't be required to do work that bores you. What you are saying has some truth to it. For example, some school subjects are not very interesting. However, we go to school to become educated, not entertained. If you want to become successful, you must be able to read, write, and calculate. You must master difficult subjects. The same applies to work. When we go to work, we learn skills and we learn to accept responsibility. You can be successful at school and work if you are willing to make the effort. Keep in mind that without an education and work skills, it is likely that you will be forced to make money by engaging in unlawful activities. This will eventually destroy you. Your life doesn't have to end in that way.

VP4. Counseling is stupid. I don't have any problems. Counseling can't help me.

SR4. You're annoyed because you think that counseling isn't necessary. You believe that you don't have any problems requiring counseling. You're right about one thing. Counseling, all by itself, can't help you. If you are really convinced that you don't have problems, then in your mind, this is true for you as well. However, because someone says or even believes that he or she doesn't have problems doesn't really mean this is so. A person can deny that he has problems, but they can still exist—even if we don't want to admit them. If you do nothing, the problems will not get better. They will more than likely get worse. Counseling can't help you unless you put some effort into it. Counseling can only be helpful if we are willing to make the effort to overcome life's difficulties. If you are willing to accept help, you have a better chance of being successful. It is obvious that you have had many difficulties up to this point. It only makes sense to give counseling a chance. However, the decision is up to you. No one can make you benefit from counseling if you choose to reject it.

VP5.   Social workers don't really care about you. They just say that. They get paid to do their job. They just do it for the money.

SR5.   You don't trust social workers when they tell you that they care about you. You believe that they do their job just because they get paid. It's true that social workers get paid to work with you. However, they would get the same pay whether they went out of their way to help you or not. People who work with you could make their money more easily by telling you what you want to hear. They actually make it more difficult for themselves by confronting you and telling you what they think is in your best interest. So, if people were just doing it for the money, why would they bother to take the risk that you would disrespect and even "go off" on them when they tell you the truth? Think about it. People who really care about you are the ones who take the risk of trying to help you. They will tell you what they really think is in your best interest. This has nothing to do with money. It has to do with caring.

VP6.   Whatever happens to me is my business. Adults don't have the right to get into my business even when I make mistakes or cause problems.

SR6.   You resent adults for butting into what you think is your private business. You think that even if you are having problems that are messing up your life and the lives of other people, that this should not be of concern to them. You're right that your life is your business. What you choose to do with your life is up to you. Just because adults give you advice, doesn't mean that they can control you. Nobody can make you do anything that you don't want to do. Concerned adults, however, have the responsibility to look out for young people. Adults have lived longer than you and they have acquired wisdom from their experience. They have a responsibility to share this wisdom with you. There are only two ways to learn in life. You can learn by trial and error and by making mistakes, which can be painful. Or you can learn from adults who have experienced life. Learning from adults can make your life less stressful and increase your chances for success.

VP7.   By having an attitude and looking hard and angry all the time, I can keep people at a distance by intimidating them. This will keep people from messing with me. This shows that I mean business and have courage.

SR7.   You believe that if you act real hard and look tough, nobody will bother you. You are absolutely right. Most people will stay away from you if you try to intimidate them. However, your attitude will be viewed as arrogance by many people who could help you to be successful. You, therefore, will alienate them.

Other people who could be helpful will only dislike you and even hate you. They may avoid openly confronting you when you disrespect them. However, they have other ways of getting revenge on you. For example, teachers can give you poor grades and fail you. Principals can suspend you, and even expel you. A boss can fire you from a job or give you a poor reference. People can refuse to give you a second chance when you make a mistake. They can get even with you, but not right away. When they get revenge, however, it could ruin your future. There is one other thing that you need to consider thinking about. If you always act hard, there are some people who will want to test you. They will want to enhance their reputation at your expense. This only leads to fighting and even killing. Is this how you want to live your life?

VP8.   If I act hard or tough, it shows that I am "the man." Exterior toughness and an attitude are signs of real manhood.

SR8.   You believe that being hard and acting tough gives you respect and makes you a real man. External toughness can certainly be intimidating and make you look like you are in control. However, this does not really make you a man. To be a man requires much more than beating up or intimidating other people. Being a man means having enough self-control to get yourself educated so that you can make it in society. A real man is able to get a good job, pay his bills, and help support his wife and children. Boys "go off" and disrespect others pretending that they are really tough. All this does is get you into fights and cause you to be charged with assault and maybe even go to jail. Is this manhood?

VP9.   If something is difficult, I shouldn't have to do it. Success should come easily and without a lot of effort.

SR9.   It is frustrating when we have to work at something that is difficult. Sometimes we cannot achieve what we would like, despite our best efforts. However, if we set our mind on accomplishing something, we can often do much better than we think we can. Keep in mind that anybody can do what is easy. People who are successful are able to do things that they dislike diligently and with excellence. You will find that people who are successful are hard workers and have good self-control. They are able to train and to work hard to obtain valuable goals in the future. In fact, many successful people have challenging, not easy, lives. They work hard to develop their talents. This is why they become successful.

VP10. If I try something new and I fail, then I would look weak and stupid. It is better to avoid making the effort because failure is humiliating.

SR10. It's scary to try something new when we can't be sure that it will turn out successfully. Trying is risky, especially when you have failed in the past and you expect to fail again. It's painful to face the fear of failure and the hurt that goes with it. However, if you never try, then you certainly will never have the chance to be successful. There is no humiliation if you try and fail. It takes courage to face challenges and to try to overcome them. Stupidity, weakness, and giving up on yourself are humiliating.

VP11. If someone disrespects me in front of others, then I must challenge them and fight so that I don't look like a "punk." If others think that I am weak and wimpy, then this is so. This would be too embarrassing for me to handle.

SR11. It can be embarrassing when somebody disrespects you in front of your friends. It is true that some people will think that you are weak if you don't "go off" on the person who "dissed" you. However, if you choose not to fight or to get revenge, you are actually being strong. You are preparing yourself to be a civilized member of society. If you want to get even, you need to use the law, not your fists or weapons. Fists should only be used as a last resort when you truly have to defend yourself. It takes courage to do what is right and not give in to what your so-called friends think you should do.

VP12. Criticism is always a put-down. People who criticize you are out to get you. Friends don't confront you with your mistakes or weaknesses.

SR12. You get angry when people point out your mistakes. You think that they do this to make you feel foolish. It is true that there are people who try to put you down to make themselves look good. However, this is not real criticism. Real criticism comes from people who care about you. They point out your mistakes so that you can learn and not make them again. People who give good criticism even make suggestions on how you can do better the next time. Such criticism can be helpful to you and your future. Without good criticism, it is difficult to learn and to improve your performance. This is why we have teachers, social workers, and other helping adults. Friends can help also if they criticize you in the right way.

VP13. Being _____ (Black, Hispanic, Asian, etc.) means I have no chance. Life is controlled by white racists. They always try to keep us down. There is no sense trying, because white people control everything.

SR13. You are feeling hopeless and angry, because you believe that racism will keep you from having a chance to be successful. You are right about some people being racist. It is true that some people are against minorities and believe that they are inferior and incapable of learning and being successful. Some people believe that minorities are stupid and that most of them are on welfare and are criminals. If you choose to give up, you will be giving white racists what they want. You will be supporting what they want to believe. Are you going to let this happen? You know that there are many minorities who have been successful. You must decide whether you want to be like them or let the racists defeat you. It's your choice.

VP14. If someone does something wrong, that means it's OK for me to do something wrong as well.

SR14. It makes you angry when other people do bad, unfair things, especially when no one catches them and they are not punished. You believe you shouldn't be penalized either and resent it when we expect you to do what is right. Keep in mind, however, that doing the wrong thing can backfire on you. It's a lot easier to do the right thing and not be looking over your shoulder all the time. When you do the wrong thing, you will eventually get caught and you will pay, maybe big time. This could ruin your future.

VP15. The system (foster care) "owes" me because I'm not living with my family.

SR15. You are feeling hurt and angry because your family let you down. You believe that you have a right to live in a caring family. You have a point. Unfortunately, we can't give you a real family. We (institutional staff) *can* give you some of the gifts that a family provides to its members. We can teach you right from wrong and help you to respect yourself and others. One of the lessons a caring family teaches its members is that nobody is "owed" success. You can only overcome problems and achieve successfully by working at them. Success is *earned*, not freely given.

As you will note, the SR challenges begin by identifying the child's thought and the feeling associated with it. The SR challenge then acknowledges and gives some credence to the child's perception. As noted earlier, there are two reasons for this, First, there is some truth to the child's view, even though his or her thinking is generally counterproductive. Second, by acknowledging that the child has a point, it makes it more likely that you will be seen as being empathetic rather than one of the "enemy" who must be defended against at all costs. This approach increases the likelihood that the child will be less resistant and defensive. Therefore, the possibility that the SR message will be received and integrated into the child's thinking increases significantly.

For example, VP1 is, "Parents, teachers and social workers have messed me up. They didn't look out for me. They are responsible for my problems." The SR challenge to this first identifies the child's feeling ("You're angry") and the thought associated with it ("because you think that your parents, teachers and social workers didn't help you when you needed it and now there are major problems in your life"). Following this, you would then affirm that what the child feels and thinks makes some sense ("What you are saying has some truth to it. Some adults did not look out for you in your early years. This is partly responsible for your problems."). After this demonstration of empathy, new, forward moving thinking is then presented as a replacement for the violpathic ideation ("However, there is nothing that you can do about their past failures. You must now choose to be consumed by hurt, hatred, and resentment or try to move forward. If you make the effort, you can overcome your problems and you have a chance of being successful.").

As you can see, teaching the child to think productively requires the capacity to listen and to empathize as well as providing cogent advice on how to look at life in a more realistic and optimistic fashion. While this task is not easy, it is quite doable. By using this method, many of the barriers to personality growth can be surmounted and real, sustaining internal change will occur.

Once you have laid this foundation, you can use behavioral methods (discussed in the next chapter) to teach these youngsters the needed skills to cope successfully in mainstream society. While behavioral approaches have been shown to be effective in helping wayward young people [Ford 1996; Izzo & Ross 1990; Garrett 1985], it is our belief that establishing and maintaining a viable relationship and cognitive restructuring are the essential components upon which their potential success is based. Unless these youngsters learn to trust adults and change their thinking about themselves, other people, and life, they are not likely to be receptive to the learning and acquisition of new skills. Hence, stable and lasting changes are not likely to occur. While behavioral interventions are valuable, these are only likely to be successful if angry, despairing youth are motivated to cooperate in using them. The adult-child relationship, in conjunction with a mentally healthy outlook, is the lynch pin upon which the viability of any of these approaches rests.

7
Changing Antisocial Behavior to Prosocial Behavior

Behavioral techniques, used in conjunction with a strong adult-child relationship and cognitive restructuring, have been shown to be effective in the rehabilitation of antisocial youth [Ford 1996]. Besides developing a sense of trust and a more productive orientation toward life, it is important that these youth learn those behaviors which will enable them to interact appropriately and achieve success in mainstream society. Even if the child trusts you and you are able to help him to change his counterproductive views, he must know how to act properly. Again, this is not a task that is easily accomplished. Angry, despairing young people have, over the years, developed bad habits and negative patterns of behavior that are difficult to change. In fact, making these alterations goes against their natural grain. They are used to "going off" easily, giving in to their impulses, and taking the path of least resistance. Moreover, some of these young people are addicted to nicotine, drugs, and casual sex. For many, immediate gratification and pleasure have taken precedence over self-control and striving for more valuable long-term goals. Giving in to sloth, sensual gratification, and emotion has become consistently habitual, and therefore, is not easily altered.

Anyone who has studied behavioral psychology knows that behaviorists contend that what follows an act determines whether that act will be repeated. If the behavior produces beneficial or pleasant results, it is likely to occur again and again, particularly if there are no negative consequences to counteract this. This is exactly what causes major problems for angry, despairing youth. Many of their negative behavioral patterns have, in essence, produced short-term, immediately beneficial results. For many, this leads to deeply ingrained bad habits that are difficult to overcome. Even though these negative behavioral patterns are harmful in the long run, despairing children couldn't care less about this. Immediate pleasure, satisfaction, and the avoidance of facing adversity are more rewarding to them than valuable long-term goals that they might never achieve.

A basic example of negative behavior patterns that need to change can be the personal maintenance chores most children and adults do on a daily basis, but which abused, neglected and abandoned children may have never learned. Brushing you teeth with toothpaste, putting on clean clothes (especially clean underclothes) daily, and maintaining a relatively tidy living space are all learned behaviors. The children we work with frequently ignore these tasks because they were never consistently taught or because of the violpathic ideation, "I'm worthless, so why bother." Helping a child change these patterns by teaching good hygiene and consistently rewarding their efforts will result in increasingly positive socializing experiences and eventually higher self-esteem.

One child we worked with always wore a hooded jacket that covered his head and most of his face. Underneath this jacket, his clothing was dirty and smelly. His hair was dirty and matted and his skin was dry and dirty as well. He had never been taught simple grooming techniques. Initially he resisted any change. However, when changes were encouraged and rewarded, he eventually gave up his hooded clothing and allowed people to see him because he felt better about himself.

When a person is without hope, immediate pleasure seeking helps to "take the edge off life." The buzz or high from drugs and alcohol, the pleasant sensations associated with casual sex, and staying in bed on a cold morning rather than going to school on time take precedence over the more rigorous tasks requiring self-control. Why deny yourself these pleasures when you believe that your future is bleak no matter what you do? Why invest your psychic and emotional energy in more difficult, time-consuming tasks when you believe that you'll be a loser in the end? Moreover, why give up your attitude when, in the short run, this helps you to distance yourself from people and keeps them from confronting you or requiring you to make a substantial effort? If you act or look menacing, it's less likely that people, including adults in authority, will trouble you. Further, if you impulsively "go off," this might even enable you to dominate or to avoid a potentially threatening situation.

A good example of the latter occurred with an 18-year-old young man who had a history of being sexually abused by his mother's boyfriend. This young man not only had emotional problems but he was severely learning disabled as well, particularly in the areas of language and reading. Despite being in an eleventh grade class, he could only read at about a third grade level. This young man was chronically angry and could become markedly oppositional when threatened. In fact, he was quite skilled at being intimidating. Unfortunately, a new teacher who was unfamiliar with his many problems did not understand this. Not realizing his severe reading handicap, she called upon him to read a section from a textbook in front of the entire class. Needless to say, this was a major mistake. This young man immediately "went off," blaming the teacher for not giving him clear instructions about the section that he was supposed to read. This made-up excuse and his outburst caused him to not only be removed from the class but led to a suspension. While many people would view this as a punishment, which would make it less likely that such behavior would occur again, this is far from the truth. "Going off" was beneficial. It enabled this troubled young man to avoid the shame and embarrassment of trying to read in front of his peers. In fact, it is quite likely that without counseling, this young man would do this again, should the same demands be placed upon him.

As this example shows, what follows a behavior determines whether that behavior is repeated and persists. Moreover, it shows that we must look inside the child to determine what motives are the driving force behind his actions. For a youngster who has been reared by caring parents, teacher disapproval and suspension might be a true punishment making it likely that this behavior would not occur again. For our 18-year-old, however, these were actually a reward that enabled him to escape an embarrassing situation. While the principle of "What follows a behavior determines whether it is repeated" has validity, we must really know the child if we are to determine what is truly rewarding and punishing to him.

Keep in mind that motivating the child so that he or she wants to change is the key in successfully applying behavioral methods. Remember, abused, angry youth behave as they do because this is immediately beneficial to them. They won't put forth the needed effort to obtain more valuable long-term rewards (e.g., high grades, a diploma, college entrance, etc.), because they have neither acquired the self-control or the skills needed to attain these. We must provide those incentives that will motivate them to change. It is important that these incentives be highly desirable. They must be powerful enough so that the child will be willing to not only make the effort but will refrain from engaging in the negative behavior of the past. In other words, the rewards have to be more desirable than the pleasures or comforts associated with the bad habits. If they are not, then it is unlikely that the child will be motivated to change. He or she will simply continue in the hopeless, self-defeating cycle that has governed much of his or her life.

While finding appropriate incentives is a key component of affecting behavior change, identifying those that are truly powerful enough to bring this about is a challenge. If we really think about this, however, there are a number of rewards and privileges that can be used to motivate troubled youngsters to try and improve their behavior. For example, trips to a fast food restaurant, a ball game, or an amusement park can be made contingent on behavioral improvement. The extras of life, like brand-name clothes and tennis shoes, special foods (e.g., pizza and "junk" foods), purchasing or renting a video, or getting a driver's license can be powerful incentives. There are a number of potential incentives that we often provide on a noncontingent basis that could serve as rewards for acquiring and maintaining self-control, making good choices, and persisting in the face of adversity.

Ask the youngster directly what she would like to earn. Also, observe the child's reaction when discussing events or sought-after privileges; this can give you some insight into what might be of value to her. Some young people would work diligently and persistently to receive tickets to a ball game, while others might improve their performance to obtain a visit with their grandparents or an extended visit with relatives or a wayward parent who is trying to get her life back on track. There are numerous rewards that we can offer. Identifying those that are of value to your child, establishing an agreement on what needs to be done to earn them, and making sure that you can promptly deliver the rewards are the keys to successfully implementing behavioral psychology.

Using Contingency Contracts

A behavioral approach that we have found to be particularly effective with our young people is the use of contingency contracts. Contingency contracts are written agreements between the child and the helper. They specify what is expected from the child and what rewards will be given for behavioral improvement. The use of contingency contracts is valuable for four reasons. First, they require that the child make a commitment in writing. Second, a commitment in writing is much more likely to be perceived as being binding. Third, a written contract is likely to be more specific and less ambiguous than a verbal agreement. Fourth, a written contract is much more likely to hold the child accountable and to facilitate the acceptance of responsibility. You will need to take the following steps to implement contingency contracts successfully:

- Identify the specific reward(s) for which your child would be willing to work.
- Specify the behavior(s) needed to receive the reward. Make sure that the behavior(s) is clearly defined so that there is no room for disagreement about what is expected. For example, avoid making statements like, "Do good in school," or "Behave responsibly at your place of residence."

Such statements are ambiguous and could cause arguments later on as to what "good" and "responsibly" mean. Rather, state that you want the child to "attend school every day on time for the entire week," or that you want him to "make the bed, dust and vacuum the room, and put his clothes in the closet every day." The more exact the behavioral requirements, the more likely it is that the youth will understand and comply appropriately. Moreover, this makes it less likely that disagreements, defensiveness, and a strained relationship with your child will come about.

- Once you have come to a verbal agreement on what the reward will be and what must be done to obtain it, put the agreement into written form—a contract. The contract should be typed (this makes it look official) and contain the following:

  - An overall, official title written/typed with capital letters on the top such as: A CONTRACTUAL AGREEMENT, BEHAVIOR CONTRACT, or CONTRACT FOR BEHAVIOR CHANGE
  - Beginning and ending dates of the agreement
  - The behavior(s) to be increased (e.g., complete all homework assignments, wash dishes every day, etc.)
  - Any negative behavior(s) to be decreased (e.g., no school suspensions during the fourth quarter, no cussing at staff or adults in authority, etc.)
  - The reward(s) to be earned for appropriate behavior and, if needed, what percentage or how much (specific numerical count) compliance is necessary to receive them
  - A penalty clause (this can be optional) for the failure to fulfill terms of the agreement (e.g., if _____ arrives late for school, she will be grounded for one weekend night for each late arrival)
  - The delivery date (specific month, day, year, and time) on which the reward is to be given
  - Spaces for the signatures of all those persons who are involved in helping the child to fulfill the contract (e.g., counselor, social worker, foster parents, teacher, principal, employer, etc.)

- A place where an "official" stamp or seal can be placed, verifying the completion and witnessing of the contract
- Once the contract has been completed, have the child read it over with you so that the terms are perfectly clear. Any changes in the agreement should occur at this time. Once he has agreed, all parties should sign their names in the appropriate spaces. An official witness (e.g., someone who serves as a "notary," a secretary could serve this purpose) will then stamp or attach a seal to the contract making it final. Distribute copies to all involved persons.
- When the terms of the contract are completed, meet with the child and deliver the reward accordingly. If the terms are not met, go over the contract and either renegotiate it, making appropriate changes, or put the same contract into effect again. It might be appropriate to lower the behavioral standards to achieve the reward or to offer the option of lower behavioral standards for less reward. This might entail breaking the behavioral requirements into smaller units or steps and providing the reward in smaller amounts for each successful completion of a step or unit.

If the contract is not initially successful, don't give up. Try to determine why it did not work. It could be that the child, because of cognitive, emotional, or social limitations, needs more time or just does not now have the capability to fulfill the requirement. He or she might have bitten off too much too soon. If this is the case, renegotiation is in order. Do not get into making excuses, blaming, or other maneuvers. Focus on the child's behavior and foster a fair agreement that is likely to be successful the next time.

In the beginning, try to develop a contract that the child can successfully complete but is not too far beneath her or his capability. This will encourage a willingness to work on other, more difficult contracts. Make sure that the reward matches an appropriate output of work. You don't give a child a trip to Disney World for going to school on a daily basis. Rather, you would require clearly specified, mutually agreed-upon excellent performance over an extended period of time to earn such a reward. Be careful not to be manipulated into an unfair agreement. This can easily occur if you are strongly attached to the child and feel badly because the contract has failed. Make sure your contracts are well-balanced. In other words, contracts should be challenging but not overwhelming. They should require that the child make real progress in acquiring good character traits and needed skills. Examples of behavior contracts are shown on pp. 99-102.

One final point: When you have arrived at the point of being able to negotiate a contract with a child, you have overcome a major hurdle. Establishing a contract signifies that the child trusts you enough to not only engage in such negotiations, but that he believes that you care and will keep your promise. This, therefore, provides you with an opportunity to not only deepen your relationship, but enables you to focus on the consequences of appropriate and inappropriate behavior. During any negotiation, you and the child can discuss the pros and cons of behaving well or poorly.

When children succeed, they learn that, despite their horrendous past, they can control themselves and sustain the needed effort to gain valuable long-term rewards. Moreover, with the establishment of a successful behavioral pattern, their self-concept and prospects for the future improve. Contracts make such progress possible. They provide the incentive to replace bad habits with good ones.

Even when the youngster fails to fulfill an agreement, much beneficial learning can occur. Failure can engender productive discussions about goals and what it takes to achieve them. This process requires you to communicate behavioral expectations, set appropriately high standards, and to be willing to commit yourself to the fulfillment of promises. Your willingness to negotiate and establish more contracts, even when the child fails, is evidence of your continued belief in her or his capacity to accept responsibility and to achieve successfully.

Role Playing

Another behavioral technique that can be helpful with neglected and abandoned youth is role playing, where the helper and the child actually practice

BEHAVIOR CONTRACT

Starting Date _____   Ending Date _____
            month/day/year   month/day/year

Positive Behaviors (to be increased):

Negative Behaviors (to be decreased):

If _____ completes _____ of the
        Child/Adolescent Name   Percentage/Number

positive behaviors and decreases _____ of the
                                      Percentage/Number

negative behaviors, then _____ will
                              Name of Social Worker or Staff

_____ .
        Reward

Delivery Date: _____
                 month/day/year

Penalty Clause: If _____ fails to fulfill the terms
                      Child/Adolescent Name

of this contract, then _____ .
                              Penalty

_____   _____
  Child/Adolescent Signature   Social Worker/Other Staff Signature

        _____
            Witness Signature

SEAL

BEHAVIOR CONTRACT

Starting Date ____1/7/99____   Ending Date ____1/12/99____
            month/day/year   month/day/year

Positive Behaviors (to be increased):
  1. Arrive at school on time every day.
  2. Attend all classes on time every day.
  3. Complete all homework for the week.
  4. Turn all homework in when it is due.

Negative Behaviors (to be decreased):

  1. Being late for school and classes.
  2. Not turning in homework
  3. Being suspended.

If ____Robert Harrison____ completes ____100%____ of the
        Child/Adolescent Name   Percentage/Number

positive behaviors and decreases ____100%____ of the
                                 Percentage/Number

negative behaviors, then ____Linda Morris____ will
                          Name of Social Worker or Staff

buy Robert a pizza and take him to a movie of his choice .
          Reward

Delivery Date: ____1/13/99____
               month/day/year

Penalty Clause: If ____Robert Harrison____ fails to fulfill the terms
                     Child/Adolescent Name

of this contract, then ____his weekly privileges will be lost____ .
                              Penalty

____Robert Harrison____   ____Linda Morris____
  Child/Adolescent Signature   Social Worker/Other Staff Signature

            ____Mary Steward____
              Witness Signature

SEAL

BEHAVIOR CONTRACT

Starting Date ___5/5/99___ Ending Date ___5/12/99___
  month/day/year   month/day/year

Positive Behaviors (to be increased):
   1. Make bed and clean room daily before going to school.
   2. Be on school bus at 8:00 A.M. daily.
   3. Complete and turn in all homework for the week.

Negative Behaviors (to be decreased):

   1. No cussing or swearing for the week.

If ____Brian Owens____ completes ____two____ of the
       Child/Adolescent Name   Percentage/Number

positive behaviors and engages in ____zero____ of the
                                   Percentage/Number

negative behaviors, then ____Jim Lewis____ will
                          Name of Social Worker or Staff

take Brian to a fast food restaurant for $5 worth of food ____. If
         Reward

__Brian__ completes all ____three____ of the positive behaviors and
                         Percentage/Number

engages in ____zero____ of the negative behaviors, then
            Percentage/Number

____Jim Lewis____ will take Brian to a baseball game and
Name of Social Worker or Staff

purchase $10 worth of treats for him ____.

Delivery Date: ____5/13/99____
                 month/day/year

Penalty Clause: If ____Brian____ fails to complete homework for the
                   Child/Adolescent Name

week, then he must make up all assignments over the weekend.
                              Penalty

All privileges will be lost until these are completed and

turned in. ____.

__Brian Owens__	__Jim Lewis__
Child/Adolescent Signature	Social Worker/Other Staff Signature

__Jill Roberts__
Witness Signature

SEAL

how to cope with a social situation. What to do and say is rehearsed *before* the child faces the problem. This provides the youngster with a strategy or coping skill that he did not have previously.

Many abused young people, because they have been neglected early in life, have never acquired the ordinary social skills of every day living. Asking for things in an appropriate manner (e.g., Please, may I ....) or showing appreciation (e.g., Thank you for .... or I appreciate....) are skills that most people take for granted. Yet, many of these youngsters have never learned to use them.

You may want to demonstrate how to interact and to solve a problem with a teacher, how to ask a person of the opposite sex for a date, or even how to ask for information or make a reservation. Many young people avoid these tasks, because they are afraid of looking foolish. They don't realize that everyone feels awkward and/or foolish when they try something new. Normalizing these feelings and helping children deal with them effectively offers them a skill they can use all of their life. The adult helper might even share some of the fears that he or she faced and overcame to drive home this point. At any rate, once the child sees the value of role play, it can be an extremely valuable tool in helping him or her in the acquisition of social skills.

There are several steps that can be used in effectively implementing role playing:
- Identify all aspects of the situation with which the child must cope.
- Identify a specific strategy(s) that would likely be successful in mastering the situation.

- Role play the situation for the child. Use verbal and nonverbal behavior that would be effective. Then go over what you said and did with the child.
- Write down actual key words so that the child might be able to refer to these as practice cues.
- Have the child try the role play using the written cues.
- Make any appropriate corrections and try again.
- Once the preceding is done correctly, try the role play without the written cues. Do this until satisfactory performance occurs.
- Repeat the successful performance several times to ensure that learning has occurred.
- Try the role play in the actual situation.
- Get feedback about success or failure from the child. Make appropriate corrections, and try again if needed.

Malissa, a 15-year-old young lady who was in foster care, wanted to visit one of her relatives. However, she had no transportation to get there. Although the facility at which she was staying had a bus stop close by, Malissa had never previously taken the bus and did not know how to go about using it. In discussing this with Malissa, we talked about using the telephone book to get the number of the bus station, placing the call, telling the bus agent her location and where she wanted to go, and requesting information on the specific bus she needed to catch and the times that it was available. Malissa was first instructed to find the bus station number in the yellow pages, which she accomplished successfully. We then practiced what she would say to the agent at the bus station:

> "Hello, I'm located at _address_. Can you please tell me the number of the bus that I should catch to go to _relative's address_? (Malissa was instructed to write the number of the bus on the paper beside her). "What times do the buses leave _name of the bus stop near her_?" (Malissa was instructed to write down the times).
>
> Following this, Malissa was instructed to say, "So I take the number four bus from _bus stop location_, which leaves at

either 3, 4 or 5 o'clock to get to _relative's address_ ." (This confirmed that she had recorded the information accurately.) "Thank you for your help."

Another example is Joan, who wanted a new outfit. We practiced the conversation she would have about getting the new clothes. The planning included her facial expression, tone of voice, and body language, as well as some actual phrases. Most of these youth have poor social skills. Learning the art of a simple, short, conversation that has a beginning, middle, and an end can greatly increase their future success. Instead of walking (or stomping) into a room and demanding a new outfit, Joan practiced knocking on the door, saying "hello" and asking to speak with the adult for a few minutes. Then she practiced discussing why she needed a new outfit and engaging in a discussion with the adult. The end of the session was to include a "thank you for your time" statement. This was particularly difficult, because there was the possibility of a disappointing answer for Joan.

While these simple role plays were accomplished relatively easily, it helped these young ladies to develop a skill that they had not previously acquired. Even though these situations were not complicated ones, they are exactly the kinds of circumstances with which neglected and abandoned youth have not learned to cope. It is the ordinary, everyday situations that can overwhelm them, causing these young people to get angry, lose momentum and energy, and ultimately sabotage their best intentions. To an adult, this process may look like the acting out, defiant, and belligerent behavior that is the hallmark of abused, neglected, and abandoned youth.

These children need to learn the kinds of social skills that most of us take for granted. Obviously, all role playing will not be as easy as the ones just presented. In numerous cases, however, you will find that this can be used quite effectively in remediating the skill deficiencies of these young people.

8
Conclusion

There are many well-qualified professionals in the field who could have written this book. We have tried to put into words what many of us in the field see and work with on a daily basis. There are several key points that we have attempted to repeatedly stress throughout this work. *First, children who are abused, neglected, and abandoned, particularly in their most formative years, have been severely traumatized.* This traumatization, if ignored or not dealt with, has far-reaching implications for the development of their personality. The effects of abuse, neglect and abandonment don't just go away with the passage of time. Rather, they fester and grow like an untreated cancer, eating away at the cognitive, social, and emotional foundation upon which normal personality growth is built.

As we have emphasized, young people who develop normally have their psychological, emotional, and safety needs met in their most formative years. They, therefore, don't become locked into the negativism of the past but can use their psychic energy to master those developmental tasks of ordinary living. This is not so, however, with abused, neglected, and abandoned youth. They, unlike their normal counterparts, are yoked to the misery that has befallen them in their most formative years.

It is extremely difficult to forget or to put aside the physical and emotional pain of being molested, beaten, berated, ignored, and abandoned by parents and relatives. Those memories can, and in many cases do, haunt the children, adolescents, and even adults who have experienced them. When a child becomes a prisoner of a traumatic past, feelings of mistrust, insecurity, and even hopelessness and outright despair can be the dominant forces affecting his or her life.

It is true that people make choices and should be held accountable for them. However, as George Orwell stated in his book, *Animal Farm,* "Some are more equal than others." In other words, equality of opportunity and fairness is a myth, particularly for youngsters who have a history of abuse and neglect. Those of us who have been fortunate enough to be surrounded by caring adults and a nurturing environment are more likely to be able to mobilize our inner resources so that we can make good choices leading to success in mainstream society. We are not encumbered by the emotional baggage from the earlier years. Resentment, bitterness, hopelessness and outright hate are not the driving forces behind our decision making.

It is much easier to be rational and clear thinking when emotional "junk" from the past doesn't get in the way. It is far easier to be optimistic and to overcome adversity when you have a positive self-concept built on a history of success. While there are Horatio Alger stories of people who "pull themselves up by their bootstraps," and can make adversity in their lives a motivator for future success, these are the exception rather than the rule. In fact, if we were to closely examine the background of these exceptional persons, we would find that there were people along the way who took a special interest in them. The guidance that they provided paved the way for their success.

This leads to a second important point that we have repeatedly made throughout this book. *Abused, neglected, and abandoned children need caring adults.* They absolutely must experience the consistent love, nurture, and dedication of at least one caring person. Without this, no bonding or connectedness with the human race will ever occur. It is love, nurture, and caring, particularly in the worst of times, that will help the child to break away from and overcome a horrendous past.

When children fail to bond with truly caring adults, their personalities become twisted. They become not only mistrusting, but they have no feelings or empathy for others. Moreover, they become moral misfits whose only concern is to keep themselves from being arrested and incarcerated by the legal system. Unless the child trusts and wants to please the significant adults in his life, he can never learn from them. His thinking will become jaded, perverted, and extremely egocentric, and his behavior will become antisocial and even dangerous.

A child who bonds and trusts can acquire hope. He can learn to view life realistically and positively, not always, but sometimes. He can learn to make good choices rather than to become a creature of impulse, sloth, and sensual gratification. He can learn to overcome his street mentality and develop those social skills needed for success in mainstream society. Moreover, the child who trusts and bonds with a caring adult will want to do just that. He will be motivated to change and to try to overcome the challenges facing him. Without this motivation, no growth can occur. The child must believe that he not only has a chance for success, but that if he invests the effort, he is likely to achieve it. Again, this is not likely to occur without the consistent nurture, support and advocating of a caring adult.

Finally, there is one last point that we would like to emphasize. *There is no quick fix to solving the problems of unfortunate youth.* We can hire more police, build more and bigger prisons, and even incarcerate children with adult felons. We can require the divisions of social services and juvenile justice to develop new programs, policies, and bureaucracies. We can put together boards of eminent professionals, business persons, politicians, and community members to study the problem and make recommendations. We can condemn, criticize, blame, and chastise parents, professionals, community members, law enforcement, politicians and the court system. None of these endeavors will work.

Unless we clearly identify and acknowledge the root causes of youthful fury, despair, and antisocial behavior and make available the trained personnel and resources needed to deal with this, the problems will continue. It is not enough to become indignant and emotional about some highly publicized criminal violation by a juvenile offender. Publicity in the newspapers and on national television only temporarily sensitizes us to this growing problem. If we really want to stop such behavior, then, like a good parent, we must consistently and persistently advocate for those programs, services, and resources that will truly enable these young people to have a chance of succeeding in mainstream society.

References

American Psychiatric Association. (1994). *Diagnostic and statistical manual of mental disorders* (4th ed.) [DSM IV]. Washington, DC: American Psychiatric Association.

Azar, B. (1995, November). Foster children get a taste of stability. *American Psychological Association Monitor*, pp. 8-9.

Crime time bomb. (1966, March 25). *U.S. News and World Report*, pp. 28-36.

Ford, H. A. (1996) *Maryland can prevent youth violence: A special report.* Baltimore, MD: Advocates for Children and Youth.

Webster's New Collegiate Dictionary. (1949). Springfield, MA: G. and C. Merriam Company.

Garrett, C. J. (1985). Effects of residential treatment on adjudicated delinquents: A meta-analysis. *Journal of Research and Delinquency, 22,* 278-308.

Guerra, N., & Slaby, R. (1990). Cognitive mediators of aggression in adolescent offenders: 2. Intervention. *Developmental Psychology, 26,* 269-277.

Izzo, R. L., & Ross, R. R. (1990). Meta-analysis of rehabilitation programs for juvenile delinquency. *Criminal Justice and Behavior, 17,* 134-142.

Lavin, P. (1998) *Profiles in fury: The psychodynamics of angry youth going "bad."* East Rockaway, NY: Cummings and Hathaway.

Lavin, P. (1996). *Working with angry and violent youth.* Columbia, MO: Hawthorne Educational Services.

Masten, A. S., & Coatsworth, J. D. (1998). The development of competence in favorable and unfavorable environments: Lessons from research on successful children. *American Journal of Orthopsychiatry, 53*, 205-220.

Shealy, C. N. (1995). From boys' town to Oliver Twist: Separating fact from fiction in welfare reform and out-of-home placement of children and youth. *American Psychologist, 50*, 565-580.

Snyder, H. N., Howard, N., & Sickmund, M. (1995). *Juvenile offenders and victims: A national report.* Washington DC: Office of Juvenile Justice and Delinquency Prevention.

Tate, D. C., Repucci, N. D., & Mulvey, E. P. (1995). Violent juvenile delinquents: Treatment effectiveness and implications for future action. *American Psychologist, 50*, 777-781.

About the Authors

Paul Lavin, Ph.D., received his doctorate from the University of Maryland in 1971. He is currently Assistant Professor of Psychology at Towson University. Dr. Lavin is a practicing psychologist who has written extensively on working with problem youth.

Cynthia Park, M.S.W., CCDC, did her undergraduate work at Beloit College in Wisconsin, where she received a Bachelor's Degree in Sociology. She went on to pursue a Master's Degree in Social Work from the University of Maryland's School of Social Work and Community Planning. Ms. Park is also a Certified Chemical Dependency Counselor. Her professional career includes work with pilot programs offering youth diversion and university student alcohol and drug programs. As a Child Protective Services Worker, she conducted investigations of alleged child abuse and neglect in a large metropolitan community outside of Washington, D.C. Currently, Ms. Park is Assistant Director of a residential group home for emotionally disturbed children.

From CWLA Press

Firesetting Children: Risk Assessment and Treatment

George A. Sakheim
& Elizabeth Osborn

Intended for use by psychologists, clinical social workers, and other mental health professionals, Firesetting Children describes the personality, behavioral characteristics, and family background variables that have been consistently and positively associated with firesetting behavior. It shows how a firesetter risk evaluation may be performed to allow for important distinctions to be made between juvenile firesetters and nonfiresetters and between low-risk match players/curiosity firestarters and high-risk/pathological firestarters.

To order *Firesetting Children: Risk Assessment and Treatment*

1994/0-87868-579-0/#5790 $14.95

Write: CWLA   Call: 800/407-6273
         P.O. Box 2019   301/617-7825
         Annapolis Junction, MD 20701
e-mail: cwla@pmds.com   Fax: 301/206-9789

Please specify stock #5790. Bulk discount policy (not for resale): 10-49 copies 10%, 50-99 copies 20%, 100 or more copies 40%. Canadian and foreign orders must be prepaid in U.S. funds. MasterCard/Visa accepted.